The Wines of the *Languedoc-Roussillon*

WENDY GEDNEY

First published in the United Kingdom in 2014 by Vin en Vacances

ISBN 978-0-9928200-0-8

Book Production by The Choir Press

Contents

About the Author

Not that long ago I knew very little about wine. Fate brought me to the subject and opened up a new life for me, one I never imagined living and one that introduced me to people that I could never have met in my old life. And it brought me back to the Languedoc-Roussillon, this magical and very special place where I now live surrounded by vines and earning my living from and with them.

The journey began in 2001 when I enrolled on a wine appreciation course at Coventry University and without planning it I found myself five years later the proud possessor of the WSET Diploma. Not bad for a girl who left Barker Butts Secondary Modern School aged just 15 and went to work on the hanky counter at Owen Owen department store!

What was I going to do with this diploma? I had not planned it but again fate stepped in; I was invited to be a wine teacher at Birmingham College of Food and began a very enjoyable few years teaching others about this amazing subject. I started my own wine school too and over the years have trained hundreds of people for fun and for qualifications. I loved it but I hankered for a life in France and fate stepped in again and I was invited to Languedoc where I met two wonderful wine families, the Fords of Domaine Gayda and the Bojanowskis of Clos du Gravillas. I will always be indebted to them for the help they gave me to begin my vineyard tour business Vin en Vacances.

When I began the tours I was eager to learn as much as possible about the area. I searched for a book that would piece the jigsaw together for me; surely there would be one that listed all the appellations and IGPs. I wanted to know what sort of wine is made in each village and around each town and city and in each of the departments. I wanted to know the styles of the wine allowed in each appellation and which grapes they can and can't use. I searched long and hard for such a book but none could be found so I decided to write it myself.

I am grateful to Matthew Stubbs and his wine course which I attended at Vinécole. There I studied for the Sud de France Languedoc-Roussillon Master's certificate, which filled in many gaps in my knowledge and inspired me to explore appellations I had known very little about before.

I hope this book will help you find your way to appellations, some of which you may not have heard of before, and seek out fine producers within them. There are hundreds of amazing wine makers out there and thousands of wines to discover and each year they are joined by others. So I hope you will find this book useful and I hope you will enjoy exploring this amazing place and tasting some of the most interesting and diverse wines France has to offer.

Introduction

I remember the first time I came to the Languedoc-Roussillon. It was the summer of 1990 and in those days I could hardly be described as a wine connoisseur, in fact quite the opposite. Yes, I liked to drink wine, but my taste had not developed beyond a glass of good Sancerre. It was a family holiday that brought me to the region; I was attracted by the Mediterranean climate and the 'good value' accommodation and my husband was attracted by the wine. He was the wine buff in the family and had heard that the wines of this region were undergoing great change which he wanted to discover for himself.

I had never been wine tasting at a vineyard and was very excited at the prospect of it. John had explained that this region of France was known for good value wine and quantity rather than quality, but change was afoot. He said that this place had everything you needed to make wonderful wine. The Mediterranean climate that could produce ripe grapes, many different soil types and the quality grape varieties now planted. Also with the advent of the AOC and the then fairly new Vins de Pays category introduced in the 1980s, wines were said to be greatly improving.

We were staying in the Corbières, which is a rugged and beautiful part of the Languedoc, and back then it had a great many co-operative wineries and only a few independent producers. Hardly any books had been written about the area and we didn't have much to guide us so we headed off in search of welcoming 'Dégustation' signs. In fact the first place we came upon was on the roadside just outside a village; an old lady sat there under a parasol, next to a barrel where three bottles of wine sat basking in the sun.

We stopped and my excitement built at the prospect of discovering a great wine. There were three wines to choose from; a rosé and two reds, and I was disappointed to see that no white wine was on offer. I eagerly accepted the glass of red that was offered and following John's lead I sniffed at it, expecting the beautiful aromas of ripe fruit. Instead I remember a cloud of alcohol and some very astringent-smelling cooked fruit odours. I sipped it and although these days I am used to spitting wine to avoid inebriation, on this occasion I spat it out because it tasted so rank! I looked at John, aghast. He had said that this place had everything needed to make good wine, so why was it so disgusting? 'Well,' he replied, 'you see, there's something missing. Yes, they have this wonderful terroir and better grape varieties nowadays, but it's not just these elements that make good wine. You need the right people. You need people who have passion for wine and passion for the way it's grown and made. That's been missing here for a long time, but those people will come. Already wine makers are arriving here, attracted by the climate and the price of the land. The children of the local wine growers are developing new skills and have a great passion for the place where they were born. One day the wines of the Languedoc-Roussillon will be some of the most exciting wines in France, you mark my words.' And he was right.

CHAPTER 1

Quantity to Quality

FRANCE
Paris
Lyon
Montpellier

GARD

A75

NÎMES

HERAULT

St Saturnin

TERRASSES DU LARZAC

PIC ST LOUP

SOMMIÈRES
St Drézery
St Christol

Montpeyroux

Cabrières

COSTIÈRES DE NÎMES

CLAIRETTE DU LANGUEDOC

St Georges d'Orgues

CLAIRETTE DE BELLEGARDE

GRÈS DE MONTPELLIER

Muscat de Lunel

Mejanelle

MONTPELLIER

Berlou

FAUGÈRES

PEZENAS

Muscat de Mireval

Roquebrun

ST CHINIAN

Muscat de St Jean de Minervois

PICPOUL DE PINET

BÉZIERS

Muscat de Frontignan

CANAL DU MIDI

CABARDÈS

Minervois La Livinières

MINERVOIS

MEDITERRANEAN SEA

A61

A9

AUDE

MALEPÈRE

CARCASSONNE

Quatourze

LA CLAPE

LIMOUX

CORBIÈRES

Corbières Boutenac

NARBONNE

• BLANQUETTE DE LIMOUX
• BLANQUETTE DE LIMOUX MÉTHODE ANCESTRALE
• CREMENT DE LIMOUX

FITOU

MAURY

Tautavel

CÔTES DU ROUSSILLON VILLAGES

FITOU

Lesquerde

Latour de France

AOP
APPELLATION D'ORIGINE PROTÉGÉE

Crus *Muscats*

Caramany

CÔTES DU ROUSSILLON

PERPIGNAN

Muscat de Rivesaltes

Les Aspres

PYRÉNÉES-ORIENTALES

RIVESALTES

Banyuls & Banyuls Grand Cru

COLLIOURE

SPAIN

So why did Languedoc-Roussillon produce such bad wine? To answer that question we need to understand a little bit about its history and what made this place tick. It all began 2,600 years ago with the Greeks, followed by the Romans. Julius Caesar conquered Gaul in 51 BC and we have evidence from that era that describes the wines produced around the city of Narbonne, which was the capital of Roman Gaul. The Romans knew a thing or two about growing and making wine and many of the things expounded by Pliny and the like are still practised today.

It's not until the Middle Ages that we again have recorded information about wine growing and this time it's the monasteries that are responsible for it. The Roman Empire collapsed in AD 476 and 300 years later in AD 800 Charlemagne, King of the Franks was crowned Holy Roman Emperor and under his rule Christianity flourished. The Benedictine abbey of Sainte Marie d'Orbieu was founded in Lagrasse. The Cistercians later founded the abbey of Fontfroide, also in the Corbières, and the abbey of Saint-Hilaire in Limoux, each with viticulture at the heart of them. In fact the monastic influence on wine making can be seen all over France. It was the monks who first recorded the notion of terroir and its effect on wine. They matched the terroirs to grape varieties and organised vineyards into parcels based on soil type and microclimate. They were prolific record makers and it's thanks to this that we know so much about the vineyard practices of the day.

During this time the southern part of France was called Occitania, taking its name from the Romance language of Occitane. This language is characterised by the use of 'oc' as the word for 'yes'. 'Languedoc' therefore means 'the language of oc'. Occitania stretched across the Mediterranean including the cities of Nice, Marseilles, Nîmes, Montpellier, Narbonne, Béziers, Carcassonne and Toulouse. The land of Occitania did not belong to France back then and what was to become Roussillon was part of Catalonia. Occitania was a feudal society with its many counts and lords holding allegiances in various directions. It was also full of Cathars who flourished in a society where law and order was hard to come by. The Cathar Crusade began in 1208 and raged for 20 years and was closely followed by the Hundred Years War which began in 1337. These and other religious struggles slowed economic expansion in the South whilst it flourished in the North.

The Languedoc landscape in the 15th and 16th centuries would have looked very different to that of today. Wine was needed for local consumption but vines were just a part of the agriculture here and not the dominating force they were to become. The region produced cereals and olive oil and fortunes were made through sheep and wool. Wine was mainly being produced by the monasteries which were the hotels of their day. Pilgrims and travellers, some of them important people, would be housed in the monasteries where they would be entertained with food and the local wines.

In those days wine could not become a major export for Languedoc due to the difficulty of transporting it. The major markets were in the north of France and onwards to the lucrative British, Dutch and German markets. The easiest way to get the wine up to the north of France would have been to transport it to the port of Bordeaux in the west and sail it round. However in 1241 an agreement had been drawn up between the kings of France and England that accorded special privileges to Bordeaux wines. The agreement ensured that all wine shipped from the port of Bordeaux would be made in that region. Wines from other areas could not be shipped until the Bordeaux supply was exhausted. This hardly ever happened and only 5% of wine made it from South to North.

Carcassonne

The Canal du Midi opened in 1681; it linked the Mediterranean and the Atlantic via the ports of Sète and Bordeaux. This would have enabled Languedoc wine to make its way into the market place, but the Bordeaux Privilege was not repealed until 1776. However there was a market for cheap brandy and the French government needed taxes. So in 1709 the peasants of the Languedoc were encouraged to plant vines on the poor and rocky soils, leaving the fertile land for other crops. Mainly white grape varieties were planted and the wine was distilled into brandy which could make its way along the Canal du Midi and was allowed to leave the port of Bordeaux.

Back in the 13th century it had been discovered that by fortifying a wine you would stabilise it and make it suitable for long sea voyages. The process was patented by the King of Majorca who controlled Roussillon, which was part of Catalonia in those days. A huge trade in the sweet fortified wines called Vins Doux Naturels was born. And so it was that 18th-century Languedoc was planted with Picpoul and Clairette grapes destined for brandy production and Roussillon was mainly planted with Macabeu, Grenache and Carignan for Vin Doux Naturel production.

The railway connections to the south began in 1855; Paris and the north became easily accessible, and more and more vineyards were planted in Languedoc-Roussillon. Between 1850 and 1875 France planted new vineyards that amounted to 200,000 hectares and of those plantings Languedoc-Roussillon accounted for more than 140,000 hectares. However much of the wine was being distilled and this region was making 40% of all brandy produced in France.

As Languedoc-Roussillon reached the later part of the 18th century and on into the first 80 years of the 19th century, it saw a boom in wine and brandy production. Most of it was sent north to sate the thirst of Napoleon's troops and in later years the thirst of the workers as the industrial revolution got underway. The landscape changed quite dramatically as vines replaced the cereals and were planted on the rich soils of the valley floor. Between 1850 and 1870 plantings doubled in the Hérault department. Overall in that period Languedoc had almost 300,000 hectares of vines. The peasant farmers were selling their sheep or replacing their crops with vines and large vineyard estates were expanding and taking on more workers to produce wine. Increasingly Languedoc was heading for a monoculture leaving it wide open to any fluctuations in the market or a devastating pest, should it come – and it did.

Phylloxera entered France in the 1870s when someone planted an American vine in Provence and unwittingly set the louse loose. Phylloxera had been present in North America without anyone's knowledge. It had not caused a problem to the native American vines, which are a different species to their European cousins. It lives on the root systems of the vines where it sucks the sap and eventually the European vine dies but the American vine has immunity. Once set free in Europe it headed west and came to Languedoc-Roussillon where it devastated the vineyards. No cure could be found. It was only clever thinking that got round the problem. Knowing that the American vine was immune and that only the roots were affected, eventually after much debate it was agreed that the European vine could be grafted onto American root stocks. However many of the poor peasant farmers could not afford to replant and only the large estates had the wherewithal to do so.

Throughout this time the demand for wine and brandy was increasing, especially in the working classes. But wine was in very short supply as Languedoc-Roussillon struggled to replant and get production going again. All over France fraud became rife. The feeble wine from northern territories was doctored with sugar to increase the alcohol content and cheap brandy was made from potatoes, sugar-beet and maize. The government sanctioned the creation of vineyards in Algeria and the wine was imported to France via the port of Sète. It was a dreadful time for the people of the Languedoc region. They had lost their livelihoods and were living in poverty. And as if to rub their noses in it, the port of Sète, where their wine and brandy had once left for the lucrative markets of the north, was now receiving imported wine from Algeria.

The Languedoc vineyards were the first to be replanted after phylloxera hit France. The government needed wine to quench the thirst of the nation and to get the economy on its feet again. Ignoring the concern of those who warned against quantity over quality, the decision was taken to replant with high-yielding grape varieties. With government grants Aramon and Alicante were planted on the plains and Carignan and Grenache on the better sites. So successful was this plan that by the end of the 19th century Languedoc was producing nearly half the entire French production from less than 25% of all French plantings. Languedoc was now producing industrial wine. Yields were so high that the grapes could not ripen; the resulting wine was feeble, acidic and pale and was blended with the Algerian imported wines to make it palatable.

Although demand for wine was high the market was now flooded; the price of wine plummeted by three quarters by 1901 and collapsed again in 1904. Radicals were pressing for protection and wine laws and many workers went on strike. Farmers were getting less for their wine than it took to produce and there was great social unrest which led to demonstrations in 1907. Clemenceau, the Prime Minister of the day, was a hardliner and troops were called in to keep order when 600,000 people marched on Montpellier. Shots were fired and people died but many of the soldiers mutinied and joined the protesters in their quest to be heard.

A solution to the widespread fraud had to be found and it came with the creation of the AOC which guaranteed the authenticity of the wine. The first AOCs in Languedoc were awarded to many of the Vins Doux Naturels in 1936 and coincided with the formation of the co-operative wineries. Up until then wine sales were in the hands of négociants. These merchants would buy the wine from producers to blend and sell as their own. Many people blamed the négociants for the fall in the price and accused them of dirty dealing. The co-operative wineries removed the need for the négociants by employing a wine maker and more importantly a salesman. The farmers could stop making wine altogether and take their grapes to the village co-operative. The wine would be made and sold and any profits could be shared amongst the co-operative members.

The co-operatives did not improve the quality of the wine and neither did the high demand for quantity, which was still rising. By 1926 French annual wine consumption had reached 136 litres per person and those figures include men, woman and children. There was no encouragement for growers and producers to reduce the quantity so the yields remained high. The wines continued to be doctored with richer wine from Algeria until its independence in the 1960s when wine exports ceased.

By the 1970s wine consumption in France had changed considerably; people were looking for higher-quality wine and some had stopped drinking wine altogether. The European wine lake was being filled with poor-quality overproduction from Italy and France. Growers were being offered grants to uproot the poor-quality varieties planted after phylloxera. The options were to replant with quality grapes or diversify into other crops. The result was that over 100,000 hectares of vines were uprooted. By now more AOCs had been created in an attempt to improve the image and the quality of the wines by controlling yields, terroir and grape variety.

During the 1980s the New World began to produce wine and adopted a very different approach to France and indeed Italy and Spain. Their approach was to make a fruit-led wine that was named after the grape and not the place it came from. In other words, without regard to terroir. It was a great success and more and more people began to drink wine in countries where wine drinking had not previously been the norm. Many people had found French wine labels hard to understand and French wine very dry and lacking fruit. Whereas the wines of California and Australia were fruity and easy to drink and also easy to buy. If you'd had a Chardonnay and enjoyed it then let's have another. The grape variety became the only thing you needed to think about; its provenance was often a secondary concern for many people.

France was losing market share. It needed to do something, but not at the expense of its AOC which had been formed to guarantee origin and to protect the ancient wines of France. France introduced the Vins de Pays category in 1983 and Languedoc-Roussillon started producing Vins de Pays d'Oc in 1987. This category allowed producers much more freedom to choose the grape variety and where to plant it. The New World had innovation and creativity and now so did Languedoc-Roussillon. People all over the world had caught the wine-making bug and began to look for places to make it. They wanted a place with interesting terroir in a warm climate. A place where the wine was not already famous, where creativity could be expressed and where the land was cheap. For many people Languedoc-Roussillon was that place and they came from all directions, re-christening this place the New World of France.

Soon people from other parts of France also began to buy land in Languedoc-Roussillon. People who made wine already and could bring their wine-making skills with them. They were followed by the younger generation of the local inhabitants who took themselves off to college to learn how to make wine. Many of their parents were members of co-operatives and owned vines but had no wine-making experience. They were shocked when their youngsters returned from college with ideas such as reducing yields. How would they make sufficient quantities to sell it at a good price? Surely they would go bankrupt? The answer: 'Those days are over; we're going to make quality wine that will compete on the world stage.'

The wine production in Languedoc-Roussillon today is a very different picture. There are over 3,700 wine makers in Languedoc-Roussillon. Many of them are independent producers, farming small scale on between 6 and 15 hectares, producing small amounts of high-quality interesting wines. In Languedoc much of this wine is bottled under the Vins de Pays label which has been the saviour for this region, allowing innovation to invigorate the market. Roussillon also produces Vins de Pays but AOC wines are still in the majority due mainly to the Vins Doux Naturels this region is famed for. Yes, there are still some co-operatives and bulk producers, but methods have improved and market forces have led to better-quality wine even though it is often industrially produced. Both Languedoc and Roussillon are now populated with winemakers who have a passion for the land and the wine produced on it. People who have resurrected forgotten vineyards, bringing them back to life to produce some of the most complex terroir-driven wines France has to offer.

So my husband was right. It was people that were missing. People with passion and desire for quality wine, and now they are here. Many of them are Languedoc-Roussillon born and have been joined by others from all over the world. Languedoc-Roussillon is no longer an 'up and coming' region, for it has arrived and produces some of the most exciting wines France has to offer.

CHAPTER 2

The Landscape

The Languedoc-Roussillon is scattered with hundreds of small villages, a few larger towns and a handful of cultural cities. The outstanding colour of Languedoc is green. The vines and the trees produce a lush appearance even during drought. The village houses, many of them stone-built or with faded stuccoed walls, often sport bluey-green doors, sun-bleached and faded. Punctuating the green are other hues, shutters painted faded grey or rusty red shading and cooling the pretty cottages with their pan-tiled terracotta roofs baking in the Mediterranean sunshine.

Many of the villages were once fortified, offering protection for inhabitants against the numerous invasions this area suffered in times gone by. Bearing witness to this are the lookout towers that rise from the centre of the villages or the fortified churches which in many cases are converted castles. There are a great many villages built as a 'circulade' in the shape of a snail's shell, which gave protection to the inhabitants.

Castles are strewn across this land, or at least the remains of them, with some dating back 800 years. They hark back to a feudal society, for Languedoc-Roussillon was home to a great many lords and knights. Each had their castle with the village cottages clustered around it. Some of the villages would have been enclosed within stone walls, but all that remains these days are mounds of earth where the castle stood and perhaps a few ruins. Not to be missed are the castles of Lastours in the Cabardès, Quéribus and Peyrepertuse in the Corbières and Montségur in the Ariège. They are so-called Cathar castles where followers of this faith took refuge during the crusade that eventually wiped them out.

I have found the people of the region to be warm and friendly and although in my experience their accent is a little hard to follow, my stuttering French is usually sufficient to gain me all the help I need. There is a great sense of community in the villages, helped perhaps by one of the customs I came across soon after I moved here. One morning I heard music playing over a loudspeaker. As I opened my front door to listen a voice over the tannoy said 'allo, allo', then proceeded to announce the day's goings-on. Apparently the local shop had a special offer on cheese and the fish van would be arriving at 2pm. This is a practice carried out by all the villages in the Languedoc-Roussillon. It's a great way of telling the inhabitants what is happening, such as when the water is going to be turned off or any other disruption is upcoming. A friend told me about one announcement in her village. The music that played to get everyone's attention was very sad and when the 'allo, allo' came the voice was also reverent. It told the residents that Madam DuPont had passed away; she was 86 and a daughter of the village.

The vineyards are surrounded by low-growing scrubland called garrigue which smothers the hillsides. It is the result of deforestation for the cultivation of vines, olives and grains and the rearing of sheep and goats. It is found mainly on limestone soils and is made up of a dense thicket of aromatic, lime-tolerant shrubs. These include holm oaks, juniper trees, broom, fennel and cistus, a pretty flowering bush that sports papery pink and white flowers. Intermingled with the bushes are low-growing wild herbs such as lavender, rosemary, thyme and sage. You will occasionally find chamomile, cactus and myrtle too along with wild garlic and asparagus in the spring months. Maquis is the name given to the taller shrub-covering on higher slopes such as in the foothills of the Cevennes Mountains. It was also the name given to the French Resistance fighters who hid in those forests and mountains.

Garrigue

Framing the landscape are the pierre sèche or dry stone walls built to stop erosion as well as producing a boundary. Many fine examples can be found around the village of La Livinière in the Minervois. The builders of these walls had great imagination and many of them are shaped to incorporate a bench with a curve in the wall to protect you from the Tramontane wind as you eat your lunch.

Dotted amongst the vineyards and usually alongside a dry stone wall are ancient stone shelters known as capitelles. They were used for temporary protection for harvested olives, grains and grapes. Shepherds and farmers used them as short-term refuge and places to keep tools or even the donkey should there be a sudden downpour. They are built in many shapes and sizes and the older ones have corbelled roofs and resemble an igloo made from stone.

Jenny Buske

You will also find intricately designed capitelles for breeding rabbits destined for the pot. In later years the capitelles were superseded by casots, conventionally-shaped stone huts often seen in vineyards sporting advertising for the local free paper, the *Midi Libre*. Other buildings include massets which are small, often very pretty huts used for weekend get-togethers for friends and family. They come together to enjoy a picnic and a pichet of rosé and a good talk; that's something the French people love to do!

The Lie of the Land

The vineyards of the Languedoc-Roussillon spread from Nîmes across to the Spanish border. The region contains five departments and as is traditional in France, most of them are named after the major river that flows through them.

Capitelle

The **Gard** in the far east of the region is named after the river Gardon and is home to the city of Nîmes and the nearby Roman aqueduct the Pont du Gard.

The **Lozère**, named after Mont Lozère, is the most northerly and mountainous department due to its proximity to the Massif Central. The altitude here makes it unsuitable for growing wine.

The city of Montpellier is the capital of Languedoc and is in the **Hérault** department, which is sandwiched between the Cévennes mountain range and the Mediterranean Sea.

The **Aude** is home to the medieval city of Carcassonne and also to some of the best-known Languedoc wine regions such as the Corbières, Limoux and the Minervois.

Finally we have the **Pyrénées-Orientales.** This department was created during the French Revolution and brought together two areas: the Roussillon, which was once part of Catalonia until the treaty of the Pyrenees in the 16th century, and the Fenolheda, named after the fennel that grows wild on the hills.

Languedoc-Roussillon is bordered by the Mediterranean to one side and mountains to the other, with vines spread across the plains that sweep up onto the hillsides towards the mountains. It's here where the most exciting wines are grown on a myriad of soil types, at varying altitudes and within many microclimates that offer superb growing conditions. There are some flat areas too where the soils are much more fertile and where much of the region's cheap and cheerful wines are grown. Near to Carcassonne and Limoux is the area referred to as the Atlantic corridor because here there are influences from both the Atlantic and the Mediterranean breezes. These conditions are thought to be ideal for growing both Atlantic and Mediterranean grape varieties together and proving this point the appellations of Cabardès and Malepère are a blend of at least one grape from each camp. The Roussillon

The Vine Pull Scheme

Arrachage is the French word for ripping up vines. Languedoc has seen a great deal of this since the EU initiated it in 1988 with the aim of reducing the European wine lake. Since then the French Government has continued to encourage farmers to reduce plantings using financial incentives. Over the last 15 years over 150,000 hectares have been grubbed up in Languedoc; however, this seems to be slowing down now.

stands apart, its landscape bearing little relation to that of the Languedoc and here mountains dominate the landscape. The Corbières hills are to the north and the Pyrenees to the south and sandwiched between them is the Roussillon plain that stretches inland from the sea.

Terroir

What is terroir? It's a little word with a big meaning. It sums up all the factors that the vine experiences in the environment where it grows and that in turn affect the style of the wine. Wine without the influence of terroir may simply be deliciously fruity whereas terroir-driven wines will express a sense of the place where they come from.

The two most influential factors of terroir are the climate and the soil. Also included is the altitude the vines are grown at. Is it flat or sloping land? If there is a slope, which way is it facing? Does the soil drain freely? Does the soil trap heat? Is there water nearby and, if so, is it a large body of water such as a lake or the sea or is it a trickling stream or a great river?

What is the microclimate in that place? What else is growing in the area? All of these factors affect the growing conditions for the vine and will shape the characteristics of the wine. However there is one further, highly important element of terroir. Man. How is the land being farmed? Has the terroir been matched to particular grape varieties? How have the vines been pruned and trained? What yield is being achieved? Is the land being farmed sustainably and in deference to terroir or highly commercially using pesticides and herbicides?

Until very recently all wines were named after the terroir they came from. Wines such as Barolo from Italy, Rioja from Spain and Saint-Émilion from France. All of these wines tell us the country, the region and even the town or village where they were grown and therefore the climate they grew in. It used to be very unusual to see the grape variety mentioned on the label; that's quite a recent addition. Many people think it's a great improvement to have the grape variety on the label; however, this alone will not tell you how the wine will taste. The growing conditions – the terroir – need to be taken into account too.

By way of an example, let's take an apple. If you planted an apple tree in the coldest part of your country and the same variety in the warmest part, what would the apples taste like? The apple from the cold climate might be sour and acidic in comparison to the one grown in the warmer climate which will probably be sweet, juicy and ripe. The same applies to grapes. If you taste a Syrah from a moderate climate such as the Northern Rhône and compare it to one from somewhere much hotter, such as the Barossa in Southern Australia, the wines will taste very different mainly due to the ripeness of the fruit.

Soil type also has a great influence on the wine. For instance Grenache grown on schist (compacted slate) will have silky tannins even when the wine is young but grown on clay these tannins take some time to become supple.

The overall terroir in the Languedoc-Roussillon is a Mediterranean climate with plenty of sunshine and temperatures that regularly exceed 30°C. Rainfall is low and mainly happens during the winter months apart from the occasional dramatic summer storm. Drought is the major climatic challenge and its effects are exaggerated by the almost constant wind in the region. The winds are part of Languedoc-Roussillon's personality and there are many of them, reportedly more than 11. They have an influence on many things including people and some say the winds can drive you mad. They also influence wine growing and, as is the habit of mankind, they have been christened with evocative names. The main two are **The Tramontane** and **The Marin.**

The Tramontane is Languedoc's equivalent to the famous Mistral that whistles down the Rhône river valley a little further east from here. Like the Mistral the Tramontane is a cold, dry and northerly wind and can reach high speeds of more than 60mph and blows all year round but thankfully not every day! It is, however, a welcome and healthy wind that dries the vines after rain or humidity and reduces the chances of mildew and rot. Humans also welcome it in the 30+°C days of the summer.

The Marin, as its name suggests, comes in from the sea bringing humidity and often fog, low cloud and rain. Everything becomes damp, wet and miserable. Most of the time it doesn't do the vines much good as it encourages rot and mildew. But if it's a mild episode and there has been a drought the vines can enjoy the moisture and drink from it.

The heat, drought and wind create a terroir that produces full-bodied wines with high alcohol levels. The challenge to the wine maker is keeping the balance between alcohol and acidity. As the grapes ripen the sugars build and the sugar is the potential alcohol of the finished wine. As the sugar builds, the acidity lowers and the balance between the two is key to the quality of the wine. It's important the wine maker is ever watchful, as a really enjoyable wine is fresh in your mouth due to the acidity, has delicious fruit flavours and is without an alcoholic burn; in other words, beautifully balanced.

CHAPTER 3

Wine Laws, Grapes and Wine Styles

AOC and Vins de Pays

For the average person I think one of the most confusing things about French wine is the difference between AOC and Vins de Pays. In my experience most people think AOC means top quality and Vins de Pays lower quality. This is not necessarily the case and I think it helps to understand why we have both categories. So we need a little history.

The story begins in the late 1800s during the devastation of the French vineyards by phylloxera. During this period production of French wines was considerably reduced and this led to the widespread fraudulent sales of 'famed' wines and adulteration of standard wine with cheaper wine. Something had to be done to regulate the industry so the French Assembly took the decision to delimit geographical areas and to specify where particular wines must be produced. However, it soon became apparent that France's famous wines depended on more than just the place where they were grown. Traditional practices, grape variety and wine style needed to be taken into account too, so this first attempt to regulate French wines failed.

In 1923 Châteauneuf-du-Pape producer Baron Le Roy devised a quality control system that included specified grape varieties, pruning methods, vine-training and minimum alcohol strength as well as delimiting the geographical area where the wine was produced.

As a direct result of this, in 1935 a government agency called the INAO was established and was tasked with creating the appellation d'origine contrôlée system.

Rules for each AOC were drawn up with the aim of preserving the traditional and famous wines of France that were under attack from a number of directions including fraudulent and false misrepresentation. The replanting after phylloxera had raised another danger and had the AOC not been in place there would have been nothing to stop people planting whatever grape variety they wanted on any soils, and France might have lost some of its ancient and historical wines for ever.

The AOC laws fundamentally followed the Châteauneuf prototype and the concept was enthusiastically adopted by the fine wine producers. They entered into the system to protect their name and reputation and to stamp out fraudulent wine that was effectively cheapening their 'fine' wines.

So the AOC protected the wines and also the notion of terroir, meaning that the resulting product cannot be reproduced outside its territory. When you buy an AOC wine it is regulated in terms of where it grew and the grape varieties used to make it. It must also have 'tipicity', a French word meaning the wine tastes and looks as you would expect it to. For instance, if you buy an AOC Minervois it should taste of a Minervois and not a Bordeaux, Corbières or something else.

The AOC has achieved what it set out to do. It is a protectionist system and therefore must disallow innovation and creativity. It guarantees the wine's provenance and that it conforms to the AOC rules but it does not guarantee quality. Yes, it is a Minervois, for instance, but not necessarily a good one.

In the 1980s the New World, in particular California and Australia, began to market their wines into Europe and France began to lose market share. There were many reasons for this but one of the major factors was that New World producers did not name the wine after the terroir but instead after the grape variety. People found it a lot easier to buy wine this way, not realising that it is climate plus grape variety that produces a wine style and not grape variety alone. Clever marketing!

The New World initially chose a very limited number of grape varieties and these have become known as 'international varieties'. They are: Syrah/Shiraz (same thing), Cabernet Sauvignon, Merlot, Sauvignon Blanc, Pinot Noir, Chardonnay and Riesling. Just seven grape varieties out of over 1,000 to choose from. This approach simplified everything and also did a lot of good for the industry of wine making because more and more people began to enjoy wine. People from countries where wine drinking had not been part of the culture were now regularly enjoying a glass of wine. People who had previously been cider or beer drinkers began to drink wine. No longer did you order your glass of choice by terroir; it was all done by grape variety, and more often than not the choice was one of the seven international varieties.

In the 1980s Languedoc was still trying to shrug off its reputation for quantity over quality and the government was looking at ways to improve this situation. The Vins de Pays category was created in 1983 and Languedoc embraced it in 1988. The aim was to improve wine quality but VdP was also seen as a weapon with which to fight for market share against the New World wines. Certainly the VdP category had rules, but it was more flexible than the AOC criteria and importantly it allowed the use of the seven international grape varieties. So initially, production was single varietal wine using the international varieties people had become familiar with. The Languedoc wine was cheaper to produce in comparison to other parts of France, mainly due to the cost of land, and could be sold at competitive prices.

As the years went by things began to change. Whereas AOC was seen as protectionist and stilted innovation, the VdP category allowed people to experiment. More and more wine makers embraced the VdP category and used it to label some of their finest wines, often because their wines broke the AOC rules in some way, such as grape variety or terroir. The Vins de Pays designation attracted many new wine makers to Languedoc, many from Australia and New Zealand, resulting in the region being dubbed the New World of France.

The European Union adopted the AOC model and adapted it for use in all European wine-producing countries. They placed it into a three-tiered pyramid supposed to order the wine in terms of quality: the bottom tier was table wine, the second tier for VdP and the top tier for AOC. In reality an AOC designation on the label merely guarantees the origin of the wine and not the quality and VdP can mean anything from cheap and cheerful to some of the finest wine this region has to offer.

In 2009 the EU standardised the names of the categories of wine across each EU country. The three-tiered pyramid remained but the category names were changed. For France this has resulted in the following:

Table wine has become **Vins Sans IG** – Wine without Geographical Indication, which means it can come from anywhere in France. With the change, Vin du Table has been renamed **Vin de France**.

Vins de Pays has become **IGP** – Indication Géographique Protégée, or Protected Geographical Indication, meaning the label must state where in France the wine was grown. This can be regional, departmental or zonal.

AOC is now known as **AOP** (Appellation d'Origine Protégée) – so instead of being controlled it is now protected. The use of AOC is still allowed and some parts of France have decided to stick with it but Languedoc-Roussillon has moved to the new labelling.

Cru

Cru is a French term that usually refers to a vineyard or vineyard area that is officially recognised as being superior. In Languedoc-Roussillon Cru wines are prestigious and tend to be ranked higher and although there are currently only 4 in existence this will change as time goes by.

The Wine Makers

The wines of the region are produced by a variety of businesses including récoltants, co-operatives and négociants.

Récoltants plant the vines, care for them, pick the grapes, make and mature the wines and sell them and therefore are responsible for *every* step of the process.

Cave co-operatives are usually owned by the members. The grape growers are contracted to grow the grapes, harvest them and bring them to the cave where they need to meet the standards set by the co-operative. Each has its own criteria and in some cases these are very strict with the aim of producing a range of wines at different quality levels. The region used to be dominated by co-operatives but many found it difficult to compete in a world that is demanding higher quality and have gone out of business.

Négociants are businesses that make wine and/or buy wine from récoltants and co-operatives who have made the choice not to bottle all or any of their production. The négociants will blend and bottle the wine under their own labels and usually sell the wines in large quantities to bulk retailers such as supermarkets.

Grape Varieties

The majority of red AOP wines are made using **Syrah, Grenache, Mourvèdre** and **Carignan**, either just two or three or all four but never just one. There are a handful of appellations that insist on the use of Atlantic (Bordeaux) grapes such as **Cabernet Franc, Cabernet Sauvignon, Merlot** and **Malbec** (often called Cot). They are, however, always blended with at least one Mediterranean grape such as Grenache or Syrah. There is also an old southern France grape called **Cinsault** but unfortunately plantings are in decline. It is a large, plump grape with thin skin making it ideal for making rosé wine. It's also delicious straight off the vine and eaten with cheese!

Of all the above varieties the one that is anonymous to most people is **Carignan**. This is actually a Spanish grape and has been planted in Languedoc-Roussillon for over 100 years. It had a very bad reputation for producing tannic, acidic and astringent wine. This was mainly caused by over-yielding the vine or picking too early which resulted in unripe fruit. With careful farming, site selection and picking low-yielding vines at optimum ripeness, the wine can be elegant and enticing. It has enticing flavours of ripe black cherries, violets, spice and tobacco. In the last ten years more and more producers have been offering 100% Carignan wines and many of them from old vines. Some are OK and others are truly wonderful and all are labelled as IGP because 100% Carignan is not allowed in AOP wine.

A high percentage of the vines planted in Languedoc-Roussillon are over 50 years old and vines of this age are usually prized by vignerons who are making high-quality wine. The older the vine, the lower the yield and the more concentrated the flavours.

Although vin blanc takes a back seat in AOP wines the list of white varieties is longer than the red. Many of them are local to the region; even so, the authorities decided to allow plantings of 'outsiders' aimed at improving the white wines of the region. The two main outsiders are **Marsanne** and **Roussanne**, which originate from the Rhône and have adapted well and are now allowed in many of the appellations. **Viognier** is another Rhône variety that has really taken off since its arrival in the 1990s. It's mainly used to make single varietal, IGP wines but it is gradually being allowed in some appellation wines.

Grenache Blanc and its sister **Grenache Gris** are also important. The Grenache family of grape varieties, like the Pinot family, has grapes in three colours. We have all heard of Pinot Noir, Pinot Blanc and Pinot Gris, although most people know this last one by the Italianised name of Pinot Grigio. Gris in French means grey but in actuality the gris grape is a deepish pink colour. The same spectrum of colours is found in the Grenache family: Grenache Noir, Grenache Blanc and Grenache Gris. In fact you will find many more grape families with these three colours such as Carignan, Picpoul and another obscure variety of Languedoc, Terret.

Gris grapes can be used to make very pale rosé wines or if the skins are not included in the wine-making process, you can make delicious white wines from them. None of the Languedoc appellations allow Grenache Gris in the blend but Roussillon does. It's absolutely delicious and one of my firm favourites.

The list of white grape varieties seems never-ending and includes **Bourboulenc**, an ancient variety planted here by the Greeks and found all across the south of France. It's allowed in the blend of red and white Châteauneuf-du-Pape over in the Rhône but is at its best in the white wines of La Clape, an appellation close to Narbonne. **Macabeu** (pronounced Macc-a-boo in France and Macc-a-bayo in Catalonia) is in fact a Spanish grape known as Viura in Rioja. It is mainly found in the Roussillon where it is often blended with Grenache Blanc.

Picpoul de Pinet is a delicious white wine grown around the Etang de Thau and is the perfect match for the shellfish farmed there. Pinet is the name of the village in the heart of the appellation and the grape is Picpoul, which incidentally means 'lip stinger'!

Vermentino is a Sardinian grape now allowed in many of the appellation white wines of Languedoc. Its refreshing smack of grapefruit and citrus flavour adds a zing to any white wine. You will also come across **Sauvignon Blanc** allowed in IGP wines. It's a long way from its northerly home of the Loire Valley and it often lacks the magic it displays in its preferred cool climate but there are some fine Languedoc examples, especially from the Malepère. **Mauzac** is found in the Limoux area where it plays a starring role in the sparkling wine produced there and shares the stage with **Chardonnay** and **Chenin Blanc**.

Muscat is one of the oldest grape varieties in France and was planted here by the Romans, but there are many types of Muscat. The best is called **Muscat à Petits Grain**, meaning 'small Muscat grape'. It produces wines that are very aromatic with the scent of roses, orange blossom, passion fruit and fresh grapes. Another Muscat grape is **Muscat d'Alexandrie** which is found exclusively in Roussillon.

The flexibility of the IGP category allows over 30 grape varieties to be planted in the Languedoc-Roussillon and therefore you will find many other grape varieties here. Many of the IGP wines are single varietal in the style of the New World but others are a blend of varieties that produce complexity and interest. What one grape doesn't have another does and so the wine maker can create a wine much like a chef creates a dish.

Wine Styles

Languedoc-Roussillon has a greater diversity of wine styles than any other region in France. You can find just about everything you could possibly want – apart from very low alcohol. Why? It's sugar that produces alcohol and it's sunshine that produces sugar. Therefore it's almost impossible to produce a wine with low alcohol in the heat and sunshine of southern France. The only way to do it is to pick the grapes before they are ripe. This works fairly well for whites and some rosés, but fails miserably for reds as they taste sour, green and stalky.

I know a lot of people are fearful of buying wine that has high alcohol levels but the real thing to worry about is the balance. By that I mean, does the alcohol dominate the wine or is it balanced along with the fruit and acidity? If it's balanced then you won't notice the high degree of alcohol – all you need to worry about is how much you are drinking! I prefer drinking one or two glasses of a beautifully balanced wine made with grapes that reached maturity to a whole bottle of low-alcohol wine made with unripe sour grapes. You choose!

With a few exceptions most of the appellation wines, those labelled AOP, will contain more than one grape and are therefore a blend. The appellation is written on the label and will be sandwiched between the words Appellation and Protégée. So for instance if you are buying a

---

Minervois wine the label will state **Appellation Minervois Protégée**. This guarantees the origin of the wine and tells you the terroir where it grew: Minervois.

Red Wines

In general the red AOP wines tend to be full-bodied, spicy and sometimes a little peppery with flavours of black fruits such as plums, blackberries and cherries. They can sometimes have a herbiness described as 'garrigue'. Some are smooth and elegant with a delightful freshness on the finish and some are more rustic.

Rosé Wines

Somehow a glass of rosé doesn't taste good unless the sun is shining. I only ever drink it in the summer months when it's my tipple of choice at lunch time or at the end of the day as an apéro before dinner. I prefer my rosé to be bone dry and fruity with refreshing acidity. I don't want it too complex, just chilled and delicious, and Languedoc rosé hardly ever lets me down.

White Wines

There isn't a typical style of Languedoc white wine. You will find everything from rich, full-bodied, oak-fermented wines to mineral, deeply complex, lean styles to simple fruity ones. There are some famous whites such as La Clape, where Bourboulenc comes into its own, and Limoux Blanc, which must be barrel-fermented. The main thing the wine maker needs to do when making white wine is strive to retain enough acidity to refresh you. At the same time he must harvest when there is enough maturity to give you good fruit flavour. How do you know which style you are buying? My advice is go tasting!

Sparkling

If sparkling wine is your tipple of choice then head for Limoux in the Aude region as this is the place where it all began back in the 16th century. You will find simple crisp, apple-flavoured fizz, rich complex Champagne styles and a delicious sweet and fruity style similar to a very good cider.

Sweet Wines

There are a great many ways to make sweet wine but only one of them is allowed for AOP wines in Languedoc-Roussillon and that is by fortification (see below). Those made using any other method must be labelled as IGP or Vin du France. You will come across some sweet wines made from overripe grapes that have been harvested late into October. The French term for this is Vendange Tardive (Late Harvest); however, this official term is reserved for wines produced in the Alsace and Jurançon only. There are still a few sweet wines made using an ancient method called passerillage. This involves twisting the stem of the grape bunch whilst it's still on the vine so that it can't receive any sap from the vine. The grapes will shrivel and dry on the vine and this will concentrate the sugar and produce a sweet wine with delicious acidity.

Vins Doux Naturels – Sweet Fortified Wines

Languedoc-Roussillon produces a great many sweet wines made by fortifying them during fermentation. They range from aromatic Muscats to deeply complex, darkly coloured wines similar in style to Port and Madeira.

CHAPTER 4

Wine Growing and Making

Wine Growing – Viticulture

Good wine is made in the vineyard. This is a statement that many vignerons stand by and refers to the health of the vineyard, the vines and the grapes. If you take great care of them, keep yields low and disease at bay and carefully harvest ripe healthy grapes, providing you don't do anything wrong during the fermentation process, there is every chance you will make good wine.

It is widely recognised that the finest wines are grown on poor soils with good drainage. The vine is like a weed and if allowed it will grow vigorously and produce many bunches of grapes. What's wrong with that, I hear you say; surely plenty of grapes equals plenty of wine? Over-yielding means the vine cannot properly nurture and ripen the fruit and high yields can only be supported if the vines are irrigated. However irrigation is not permitted for AOP vines after they have reached their fifth year unless there is prolonged drought. IGP wines can be irrigated and are allowed to have a much higher yield, but producers striving for quality will keep yields low and shun irrigation for many reasons. Their argument is that watering vines could dilute sugars and flavours and make the wine taste watery. Another factor is that irrigated vines become reliant on the water and do not need to send their roots deep into the ground.

Château de Rieux

Without irrigation the roots can go four or five metres deep into the bedrock in search of water and along the way pick up minerals and other influences from the soils. The wines will have complexity and interesting minerality and taste of the place where they were grown – that's terroir.

As you drive around the Languedoc-Roussillon you will see some vines are growing as bushes and others are trained along wires. Traditionally all the vines in the Mediterranean were grown as bushes, called 'gobelet' in France and 'bush vines' in the New World. This method works well for vines with a natural inclination to stand upright, such as Grenache and Carignan. Vines that are inclined to flop on the floor, as Syrah does, need support, otherwise the fruit will be shaded from the sun, which might inhibit ripening. Today we understand a lot more about growing vines and how to use the greenery (called the canopy) to help us either to shade the fruit when it's needed or to lift it up to allow the grapes to 'see' the sunlight. We also know that by opening up the canopy by using wire supports we allow aeration which helps to keep fungal diseases at bay.

The way the vines are trained will also give a clue as to how they are harvested. Bush vines have to be hand harvested; the harvesting machine needs to follow a wire.

The Vineyard Annual Cycle

The vineyard cycle begins in December or as soon as all the leaves have fallen from the vine at the end of autumn. Now the pruning can begin. The farmer must hand prune every vine and ideally this job has to be finished by the end of March before the vine begins to wake up. Pruning is an important and skilled job as it will determine not only the shape of your vine but the amount of fruit it will yield.

In spring, bud break happens and the vine awakes from its winter dormancy and sports little green buds that unfurl as each day passes. The landscape starts to change from the brown earthiness of winter to the green beginnings of spring. You will see the farmers ploughing to aerate the soils and keep weeds at bay and at this time spraying commences.

The vine is vigorous and by early spring it is flowering followed by fruit set when the tiny green flowers become minute baby grapes. From now it will take about 100 days until they are ready for harvesting.

Throughout June and July the canes are getting longer and need to be positioned on the wires if there are any. Ploughing and spraying continue. The canopy is getting larger and denser and it may be necessary to thin it in places to allow aeration and light to the fruit. The grapes are getting larger but at this stage they are still green regardless of whether they will be red, white or gris. They are also full of acid; the sugars are not there yet. That changes during August in the stage called veraison, when ripening begins. Throughout August the grapes gradually ripen, the sugar is building, the acid lowering and the colour changing. Eaten straight from the vine they are delicious.

In the Languedoc harvest begins towards the end of August for some wines and will continue into October for others. Each terroir is different, as is each grape variety. The hotter areas such as on the plains will begin harvesting earlier than those at altitude or where you find cooler microclimates. Each grape variety ripens at a different time; some are early ripeners and some late. Grapes destined for white wine are nearly always harvested first as full maturity is not needed. The wine makers want to preserve the acidity and avoid very high alcohol levels.

Harvest time is stressful for the wine maker. When to pick is the biggest decision he or she will make that year and once it is done there's no going back. Many samples are taken from the vineyard and sent to the laboratories located around the region to check the balance between sugars and acids and measure the potential alcohol. But it's not just science the vigneron relies on. I have spent many days with wine makers during this period, walking through the vines eating the grapes and deciding if they have reached that magical moment when the flavours are so wonderful you know it's time to pick.

For red wines the wine maker is waiting for phenolic ripeness and not just alcohol potential. Phenolics are chemical compounds in the grape which include the acids, colour, flavours and tannins. All these can be measured in a laboratory but many wine makers do it by tasting the grapes. Does the grape taste acidic or sweet? Are the skins chewy and leathery or soft and supple? Is the colour easily released from the skins when you rub a grape in your palm? What colour are the seeds inside? If they are green then the phenolics are not ripe, but if they are black and crunchy then they are. Some years the winemaker must wait for the phenolics to ripen and during that time the sugars will build and the alcohol potential increase. But many believe it's worth it; wine made from grapes that had good phenolic ripeness may have higher alcohol, but it will taste delicious.

Organic Wine

In 2010 Languedoc-Roussillon had the highest number of certified organic wine producers of any region of France and it is still increasing. Many of the people have been drawn here to make organic wines due to the climate and also because of the number of abandoned vineyards. They have breathed new life into them and nurtured them back to life with a high regard for the land. They produce wine as naturally as possible using low levels of sulphur both on the vines and in the wines.

Languedoc-Roussillon is an ideal place to practise organic viticulture due to the hot, dry and windy climate. One of the major battles for wine growers is against mildew and rot which occur in wet and humid conditions. In Languedoc-Roussillon rainfall and humidity are usually very low. When it does rain the Tramontane wind can usually be relied upon to dry the vines, reducing the amount of spraying needed and making it possible to avoid chemicals.

But what is an organic wine? Many of us assume it means the wine contains absolutely no chemicals at all, and by 'chemicals' we usually mean sulphur. Not true. First of all, 'organic' usually means growing the vines without the use of chemicals such as herbicides and pesticides, but sulphur and copper sprays are allowed. These are used to control some fungal diseases and as these are 'natural' products from the earth they are allowed. Until recently the word 'organic' when used for wine produced in the EU referred to the way it was grown and not the way it was made and the label would state 'wine from organic grapes'. In 2012 new regulations were drawn up to cover organic wines made and sold in the EU. The rules now specify sulphur levels must be at least 30–50 mg per litre lower than non-organic wine. In practice many of the organic wine makers I know already use much lower sulphur levels than that.

Biodynamic viticulture

Biodynamics is a form of organic agriculture first developed in the early 1920s by the Austrian philosopher Rudolph Steiner. Biodynamics is a spiritual and homeopathic approach to viticulture and takes a number of steps further than organic methods. Farmers aim to create a balanced ecosystem on their land that will generate health and fertility from the surroundings rather than using things brought in from outside. Practitioners believe that if they work with the natural forces and the rhythm of the earth, moon and stars these influences, although subtle, will help to maintain a healthy environment for growing wine. Practitioners use the biodynamic calendar, which is based on the position of the moon in relation to the constellations. The calendar is drawn up with fruit, flower, leaf and root days which are linked to which phase the moon is in. It is believed that by following this calendar the vigneron will know when it's the best time to undertake activities in the vineyard and winery.

Biodynamics also uses a complex system of herbal sprays and composting techniques and some practices can appear quite bizarre. Such as making 'horn manure', which involves burying a cow's horn filled with cow manure at the Autumn Equinox and then digging it up in the spring. When it is unearthed the manure has decomposed into a humus consistency and is stirred into water and sprayed onto the land to help regenerate degraded soils. Yes, it all sounds a bit wacky, but those who practise biodynamics truly believe in it.

Sustainable viticulture is a sort of halfway house and those who follow this practice will use some pesticides on some occasions. In France this is called '**lutte raisonnée**', meaning 'the reasoned struggle'. The farmer can decide to use chemicals if he feels they are the only resort. Some argue that being totally organic means the vines may be attacked by a disease that can be prevented, that the grapes may not be healthy *every* year and that more ploughing is necessary to keep the weeds at bay. More ploughing means more fuel consumption and exhaust emissions, but of course this does not apply to those using horse power … !

Harvesting

Hand harvesting is still the method of choice for many quality producers in the Languedoc and is a necessity where there are steep-sloping vineyards. Some appellations such as Limoux insist on hand harvesting; however, machine harvesting is carried out by many people, especially those with vineyards on flat land.

There is nothing wrong with machine harvesting and it should not be regarded as inferior; indeed there are some highly sophisticated machines that can select ripe grapes only. Machine harvesting has a lot going for it, especially speed and the ability to harvest in the dark at night or early morning. This is ideal for white grapes as you are assured of avoiding oxidation by picking when there is no sunlight.

There are thousands of wine makers and many of them farm small areas of land, making hand harvesting an obvious choice. The aim of many of the small vineyards is to make hand-crafted wines from carefully sorted fruit. They want to pick out and discard any grapes that are undesirable due to disease or over/under-ripeness and also remove any insects and leaves. A first sort can take place in the vineyards where pickers are told 'if you wouldn't eat it then don't pick it'. Then when the grapes arrive at the winery they are often sorted again before being processed. Nearly all top-quality wine is made from sorted grapes and the cost of doing this will be reflected in the bottle price you pay. But sorting is a stage that many bulk producers avoid as it is costly and will affect the price of the finished wine.

Wine Making

The biggest revolution in wine making has been temperature control. During fermentation the yeast produces heat and in the days when this could not be controlled the wine would cook and lose aromas. Before modern materials became available in the 20th century wine was produced in a huge wooden vat called foudre which would hold as much as 600,000 litres. These were not ideal because they leaked and allowed wine to oxidise and it was not possible to control the temperature. Yeast is very sensitive to temperature and on a hot day it would be very active and produce a lot of heat and workers would throw buckets of water over the foudre in an attempt to cool them down. On cold days the yeast would go to sleep and the fermentations would stop so fires were lit in the wineries to warm the atmosphere and keep the yeast working.

Wooden foudres

Concrete and fibre glass tanks

Concrete tanks were the beginning of temperature control as this material does not heat up so quickly and they are still popular today. In the 1980s stainless steel became popular all over the world, including Languedoc-Roussillon, and it is used today by many producers for both red and white wines. Temperatures can be accurately controlled and the vats are easily cleaned.

You can employ many techniques when making wine but the first step is always the alcoholic fermentation, followed by a secondary fermentation called malolactic. The first stage converts the sugar into alcohol and the second stage converts malic acid (the acid found in apples) into lactic acid (the acid found in milk). It's possible to control malolactic fermentation and prevent it occurring. All red wines go through it, but in Languedoc-Roussillon the majority of white wines will be prevented from going through this process as it must be avoided to preserve acidity in a hot climate. Maturing and blending (assemblage) if required are the next two steps and they can take place in either order. Finally maturation can happen in a tank or in a barrel, followed by bottling.

Sulphur dioxide (SO_2) can be added to the wine at various stages of the wine-making process and for differing reasons but its main function is to inhibit or kill unwanted yeast and bacteria. It should not be confused with the powdered sulphur that is sometimes dusted onto vines to protect them from mildew. Sulphur will occur naturally during fermentation and is present in small quantities even in un-sulphured wines. Have you ever found yourself with a headache after drinking only one glass of wine? It could be that the wine was over-dosed with SO_2 as this is a very natural reaction to this chemical. Wine makers don't have to add large doses of SO_2 and some don't add any at all, although there are risks with this approach. I find that the bulk producers who want to control everything to the nth degree seem to use the most.

Stainless steel tanks

Red and white wines are made differently, mainly because you don't need any colour or tannin extraction for whites.

White wine

The grapes go directly into the press, the juice is extracted and the skins are discarded.

- The juice is put into a tank and chilled to stop fermentation starting and allow the large particles to settle to the bottom of the tank and the juice clears.

- The cleared juice is fermented by adding yeast. The yeast eats the sugar and the by-product is alcohol and CO_2. The gas is allowed to drift away.

- The malolactic fermentation is allowed to happen if desired.

- The wine is now ready to mature in either a tank or a barrel and assemblage (blending) can take place before or after this step.

- After maturation it is ready to be bottled and drunk.

Red wine

- The stalks are removed and the grapes are sometimes, but not always, crushed. Crushing is when the skins are popped open to release the juice. Everything is then placed in the fermentation tank.

- The yeast is added to eat the sugar and produce heat, alcohol and CO_2. During fermentation the CO_2 bubbles up through the wine and takes the grape skins to the top of the tank, so two or three times a day the wine maker will push the skins back into the wine. He will use various methods to do this such as pumping the wine from the bottom of the tank to the top to submerge the 'cap' of skins.

- The fermentation will take an average of 30 days. When the wine maker is ready he will separate the wine from the skins and put the skins into the press to release the wine trapped in them.

- The malolactic fermentation is the next step and always happens with red wine.

- The wine is now ready to mature in either a tank or a barrel and assemblage can take place before or after this step.

- After maturation it is ready to be bottled and drunk.

There is another popular way to ferment red wines called whole bunch fermentation or, to give it its proper name, **carbonic maceration**. This method is favoured by some wine makers, especially with the Carignan grape, and produces brightly coloured red wines that can be drunk early. In order to have whole bunches the grapes need to be hand harvested and are then carefully placed in a sealed vat filled with carbon dioxide to eliminate oxygen. Normal fermentation requires oxygen but when it is excluded an intracellular fermentation begins inside the grapes, which reaches about 2% alcohol. At that point the grapes are pressed and a normal fermentation finishes off the job.

Rosé wine

There are two main ways to make rosé and mixing red and white wine together is not one of them! The first method is called **direct press** and involves pressing red grapes and then proceeding as for white wine production. This produces a pale pink aromatic rosé with a character similar to a white wine.

The other method is called **saignée**, which means 'bleeding'. It involves macerating the juice of red grapes with the skins for 4 to 12 hours, then 'bleeding' the juice off and continuing the fermentation away from the skins. This method produces a deeper pink colour and the wine often has a little more depth of flavour and body.

Barrels

Traditionally Languedoc-Roussillon wines were matured in foudre or tank but these days more wine makers are using barrels. The standard size barrel is 225 litres but you will also find a lot of producers using 500-litre capacity. The larger the barrel, the less influence it will have on the wine, and many producers do not want to overwhelm the wine with big oaky flavours.

When a barrel is used for the first time it will transfer a great deal of flavours to the wine such as spice, vanilla and sometimes toast, coffee and coconut. The second occasion the barrel is used these flavours are halved and they will continue to decrease each occasion you use the barrel. As well as flavour, barrels are used for the deliberate and controlled oxidation of the wine inside. The barrel is porous and therefore wine can evaporate through the pores and air can penetrate into the barrel. It is important to keep the barrel full to the brim so that the air that is

entering the barrel does not sit on a gap forming through evaporation as this will spoil the wine. This exchange of air and wine is called micro-oxygenation and changes the wine considerably, softening and rounding it.

Each time you use a barrel some of the pores become blocked, which reduces the micro-oxygenation. Many wine makers will keep each barrel for three years and every year retire a third of their barrels and buy another third. This way they have a three-year cycle of barrels at different ages. Each year the same wine is put into the different ages of barrel, then blended together after the maturation period. This equalises the influence of the oak on the wine.

Each 225-litre barrel holds 300 bottles of wine. A barrel of this size costs in the region of €600, so it's easy to understand why barrel-matured wine is more expensive than tank-matured.

Assemblage or blending is the art of wine making. The fermentations and various ways of maturing wine produce the components the wine maker will use to produce a delicious wine. It's a little like a chef creating a dish. The chef adds flavours with the addition of salt, herbs, pepper etc., striving for a balance that will bring out the flavours of the food and not mask them. And so it is with wine making. The wine maker will blend the different grape varieties that have been matured in various ways in order to achieve the finished wine.

So you see, wine doesn't come out of a bottle; it goes into one, and it takes a lot of blood, sweat and tears to get it in there!

CHAPTER **5**

Eastern Languedoc

GARD

NÎMES

HERAULT

A75

TERRASSES DU LARZAC

PIC ST LOUP

SOMMIÈRES

St Drézery

St Christol

COSTIÈRES DE NÎMES

CLAIRETTE DE BELLEGARDE

St Saturnin

Montpeyroux

Muscat de Lunel

Cabrières

St Georges d'Orques

GRÈS DE MONTPELLIER

Méjanelle

CLAIRETTE DU LANGUEDOC

MONTPELLIER

Berlou

FAUGÈRES

PÉZENAS

Muscat de Mireval

Roquebrun

ST CHINIAN

Muscat de Frontignan

Muscat de St Jean de Minervois

BÉZIERS

PICPOUL DE PINET

MEDITERRANEAN SEA

A9

Quatourze

LA CLAPE

NARBONNE

AOP
APPELLATION D'ORIGINE PROTÉGÉE

Crus   *Muscats*

In the Languedoc there are 35 appellations and sub-appellations (known as Dénominations Géographiques Complémentaires), which are described over the following pages. To try to simplify things a little I have divided the Languedoc in half and described the appellations contained in the eastern and western sections. These divisions are not official; they are simply my way of explaining it all.

Some of Languedoc's appellations are very well established and date back to the 1930s and others are recently formed and more will follow. The region is changing and gradually more areas are becoming defined terroirs and gaining their own appellations.

Beginning in the far eastern region of Languedoc we find **AOP Costières de Nîmes**. I'm not going to dwell for long on this AOP because although Costières de Nîmes is politically part of the Languedoc, in wine terms it's classed as part of the Rhône. This is due to the climate, soil and topography, which create wines that are far closer in style to Côtes du Rhône than to Languedoc. Even so the wines can contain Carignan which is outlawed in the rest of Côtes du Rhône; however, the soils have more similarity with Rhône than with Languedoc and contain pudding stones similar to those found in Châteauneuf-du-Pape.

The vineyards go back to the Greek times and the Romans expanded the wine trade probably when they were building the beautiful towns of Arles and Nîmes and the Pont du Gard, that wonderful aqueduct that crosses the river Gardon. Fruity red, rosé and white are produced here, although some of the reds can be rich with good depth and hold many of the characteristics of a true Rhône wine, which I always think taste slightly sweeter compared to a typical Languedoc rouge. The rosés are light and dry, traditionally well balanced and delicate, and the whites can range from light and simple to richly complex.

Côteaux du Languedoc and AOP Languedoc

In 1982 the appellation known as **Côteaux du Languedoc** was formed and spanned large areas of land between Montpellier and Pézanas and north of Béziers. In 2007 a new appellation called **AOP Languedoc** was formed to replace Côteaux du Languedoc which will be withdrawn in 2017. Until then producers have the choice to use one or the other. Before its creation Languedoc-Roussillon did not have an appellation that covered the whole area such as Bordeaux, the Loire and others have. Now with this new appellation producers can blend wines from across the entire region.

AOP Languedoc has a broader scope than Côteaux du Languedoc and covers the entire region of Languedoc and Roussillon. Therefore you would be forgiven for thinking the wines will be the same as IGP Pays d'Oc, which also spans the entire Languedoc-Roussillon region. But no, with a couple of exceptions the wine must be a blend of at least two grapes grown on AOP-delimited land. Furthermore the grapes used must be Mediterranean varieties such as Grenache and Syrah for reds and Grenache Blanc, Marsanne and Roussanne for the whites.

AOP Languedoc

The majority is red wine with much smaller quantities of rosé and white made from grapes grown on various soil types from across the entire region of Languedoc-Roussillon. The styles range from simple fruity wines to complex and interesting ones. The grapes for these wines must be a blend of at least 2 Mediterranean varieties which can be grown in the same place or a blend from across the region grown at relatively low yields.

Carthagène

Carthagène is the Languedoc version of Cognacs Pineau des Charent and is a vin de liqueur. It is made by adding unfermented grape juice to grape spirit. The grape juice does not ferment due to the strength of the alcohol in the spirit and therefore the liqueur remains deliciously sweet and depending on which grape variety is used it is sometimes chocolaty too. In Languedoc they tend to use Grenache but you will also come across other varieties such as Carignan and they are often served as an aperitif or occasionally to accompany a sweet dessert.

Sub-appellations

Languedoc's capital city Montpellier is surrounded by vineyard districts that in the past were mainly referred to as the Côteaux du Languedoc. Now, with the slow emergence of appellation hierarchy, producers in these areas can append their own sub-regional name to AOP Languedoc. For instance if you are buying a wine from Grés de Montpellier the label will state 'AOP Languedoc Grés de Montpellier'.

There are 14 sub-appellations in Languedoc which in France are known as **Denominations Géographiques Complémentaires** and nearly all of them are red wines with only a couple of white. Here is the list of the DGCs, which are all in the east of the Languedoc region:

AOP Languedoc Sub Appelations

- Sommières
- Saint-Christol
- Saint-Drézéry
- La Méjanelle
- Pic Saint-Loup
- Grés de Montpellier
- Terrasses du Larzac

- Montpeyroux
- Saint-Saturnin
- Picpoul de Pinet
- Pézenas
- Cabrières
- Saint-Georges-d'Orques
- Quatourze

Pic Saint-Loup

To discover the Languedoc DGCs let's begin close to Montpellier which is a city not to be missed and if you're looking for an interesting wine district close by the best to choose is AOP **Pic Saint-Loup.** Heading north from the city you quickly leave the suburbs behind you and taking the D17 the Pic soon looms ahead of you. It's a limestone cliff dramatically rising from the ground and reaching 648 m, and standing by its side is the smaller **Falaise de l'Hortus** at 500 m bearing a ruined castle on its summit.

Surrounding these landmarks are the vineyard of the appellation enjoying a slightly less Mediterranean climate than other parts of the region.

This red and rosé appellation is held in high regard and wines range in style from full-bodied and brooding to elegant with refreshing acidity and medium body. The air is perfumed by the garrigue that clings to the land and the wines nearly always have marked rosemary, thyme and pine characteristics. White is grown here but is not part of the appellation and is therefore either IGP or Vin du France.

Directly east of the Pic Saint-Loup appellation, in the Gard Department and bordering the Costières de Nîmes district we find the small appellation of **Sommières** where interesting red wine is made. It takes its name from the beautiful medieval village on the banks of the Vidourle river famed for its chateau and its Saturday market.

South of Sommières there is a clutch of small sub-appellations all making red wine which varies from quite acceptable to deliciously good. These include **Saint-Drézéry, Saint-Christol** and **Le Mejanelle.**

Grés de Montpellier is an appellation for red wine only and is found close to Montpellier. The wine is dominated by Grenache and takes its name from the limestone pebbles that are scattered across the district. With a few exceptions most of the vines are planted on fairly flat land and enjoy quite a hot climate that produces wines with some ageing potential.

Within the **Grés de Montpellier** appellation is the tiny sub-appellation of **Saint-Georges-d'Orques** found in the undulating hills west of Montpellier. It's in quite a built up village and the main producer seems to be the co-operative and set into this building is a circular plaque depicting a man slaying a beast. Is this France's equivalent to England's Saint George and the Dragon?

AOP Languedoc Pic Saint-Loup

Pic Saint-Loup is mainly red wine with much smaller quantities of rosé. The grapes are grown on limestone soils at reasonably low yields and must be a blend of Grenache, Syrah and Mourvèdre; a smaller amount of Carignan and Cinsault can be added but is not compulsory.

AOP Languedoc Sommières, Saint-Christol, Saint-Georges-d'Orques and Saint-Drézéry

These are appellations for red wine only grown on limestone soils with some sand in places. They are a blend of Syrah, Grenache and Mourvèdre plus a smaller amount of Carignan and Cinsault is allowed and Saint-Christol can also contain small amounts of Counoise and Picpoul Noir.

AOP Languedoc La Méjanelle

This appellation is for red wine only grown on gravel and stony soils. It is a blend of Grenache, Mourvèdre and Syrah plus a smaller amount of Carignan and Cinsault is allowed.

AOP Languedoc Grés de Montpellier

The majority of Grés de Montpellier is red plus much smaller quantities rosé grown on limestone pebbles known as Grés. The wines are a blend of Grenache, Mourvèdre and Syrah plus a smaller amount of Carignan and the age of the vines must exceed 6 years for all but the Carignan which must exceed 9 years.

AOP Languedoc Terrasses du Larzac

If you drive north taking the A75 to take a look at the breathtaking Millau viaduct that spans the river Tarn, you have entered the Larzac Plateau. It's a limestone upland grazed by the sheep that produce Roquefort, that tangy, crumbly and slightly moist cheese with distinctive green rather than blue veins that is enjoyed with a glass of anything lusciously sweet. Looking south from the plateau you will see the **Terrasses du Larzac**, a name coined by one of the finest wine producers in this area, Olivier Jullien of Mas Jullien.

The region has many villages perched on hilltops reaching for the sky or hidden in valleys and coiled around rivers. Saint-Guilhem-le-Désert is one such village and at its heart is the abbey, a jewel of Romanesque art and home to the relics of gallant knight and founder of the abbey Saint-Guilhem. The village and the abbey are part of the medieval pilgrimage to Santiago de Compostella and many people come to see the fragments of the true cross of Christ, a gift from Charlemagne.

Terrasses du Larzac is a young appellation created in 2005 for red wine only planted on the gravelly limestone slopes and terraces of this wine district in the northern Hérault. It's not all limestone though; you will also find round pebbles and sandy soils in the valleys where the mighty river Hérault meanders. There are also the much-sought-after deep red volcanic soils called ruffe found around the village of Aniane. In 2000 these soils were the battle ground for a fight between the Mondavi Empire and the local people. Mondavi's attempt to buy a small patch of land in the village of Aniane was foiled by local government officials and is a story related through the 2004 documentary film *Mondovino*.

The 23 villages that make up the **AOP Terrasses du Larzac** enjoy an almost perfect climate for producing aromatic wines with balanced alcohol and acidity. The proximity of the Larzac plateau means cool summer nights after hot days. The considerable drop in night-time temperatures of up to 25°C extends the growing season, allowing the vine to build flavours whilst maintaining acidity. These patterns of regularly occurring drops in night-time temperature are found in many famous wine-growing areas around the world and are regarded as a major factor for quality wine production.

Many talented and fine wine makers have begun to focus on this region and their wines are receiving great acclaim around the world. It will be interesting to follow the fortunes of this appellation which is set to become one of the finest in Languedoc.

AOP Languedoc Terrasses du Larzac

This appellation is for red wine only grown on limestone gravel and iron-rich reddish clay known as ruffe. It is a blend of Syrah, Grenache, Mourvèdre and a smaller amount of Carignan and Cinsault is allowed.

AOP Languedoc Montpeyroux and AOP Languedoc Saint-Saturnin

The red wine only appellations of **Saint-Saturnin** and **Montpeyroux** are close neighbours located within the Terrasses du Larzac.

The pretty village of Montpeyroux is quite large with a long straggling road that slices straight through the centre. At its heart is a good restaurant called La Terrace du Mimosa which has a fine wine list and delicious modern food. Many excellent producers have their cave in the centre of the village and just on the outskirts is a good co-operative winery. The AOP Languedoc Montpeyroux vineyards are planted on the hillsides and valleys that surround the village. It's an appellation for red wines only planted on limestone that gives powerful mineral wines of great character and many of them have ageing potential if you can keep your hands off them long enough!

The **Saint-Saturnin** appellation is west of Montpeyroux and takes its name from the village of Saint-Saturnin-de-Lucian. The village is surrounded by limestone hills and overlooked by the 'Rocher des Deux Vierges'. The 'Rock of Two Virgins' gets its name from the legend that 2 Sisters of St Fulcran came to live on top of this rocky promontory to be closer to the sky and presumably God. The village is also long and straggly and recently a very good restaurant has opened up in the small central square and is well worth seeking out. AOP Saint-Saturnin are red wines that must be made from a minimum of 3 grape varieties and are often slightly lighter and fresher than those from Montpeyroux.

AOP Languedoc Montpeyroux and AOP Languedoc Saint-Saturnin

These appellations are for red wine only grown on limestone soils at fairly low yield. They are a blend of Grenache, Mourvèdre and Syrah plus a smaller amount of Carignan and Cinsault can be included.

AOP Languedoc Picpoul de Pinet

The appellation of **Picpoul de Pinet** is located south-west of Montpellier, close to the coast. It's an oasis of vin blanc in red wine-dominated Languedoc. Only a handful of French appellations use the grape variety as part of the name and Picpoul de Pinet is one of them. It takes its place next to Muscadet sur Lie from the Loire Valley and its Languedoc neighbour Clairette du Languedoc and of course all the Muscat wines of France.

The other part of its name is taken from the village of Pinet, which you'll find slightly inland between the pretty towns of Mèze and Marseillan on the Basin de Thau. This natural saltwater lake is separated from the Mediterranean Sea by a narrow sand bar that forms a barrier between the vines and the sea. It is the only navigable étang on the Mediterranean coast and is where the Canal du Midi reaches the port of Sète.

This is the largest appellation for white wine in the Languedoc and the grape variety is one of the highest-yielding if left to its own devices. It must be harshly pruned to keep the yield low and ensure there is even and consistent ripening. To keep the yields low many producers undertake a 'vendange vert': a 'green harvest' which removes some of the forming bunches of grapes in the early months of the season.

There are two spellings of this grape; 'Picpoul' is the Occitan spelling and the French spelling is 'Piquepoul'. Either way it means 'lip stinger', presumably due to the refreshing tang that the high acidity gives this wine, making it an ideal accompaniment to the seafood that is farmed in the étang.

AOP Languedoc Picpoul de Pinet

This is an appellation for white wine only grown on alluvial and relatively fertile soils around the Étang de Thau. It is made from 100% Picpoul.

AOP Languedoc Quatourze

This appellation is for red wine only grown mainly on limestone soils. It is a blend of Grenache, Syrah and Mourvèdre and a smaller amount of Carignan and Cinsault is permitted.

AOP Languedoc Quatourze

Quatourze is a little-known appellation for red wine only and is found close to Narbonne where the vines are grown within sight of the Étang de Bages. Peering down from its eyrie is the ancient village of Bages and although this area has less dramatic scenery than its neighbour La Clape, Bages is one of the prettiest villages to visit. Just around the corner is another little gem: the village of Peyriac de Mer, also well worth a visit. The area receives little rainfall and it can be very hot in the summer but the sea breezes, when they blow, certainly cool you down; I have nearly been swept away by them on more than one occasion.

Bages

AOP Languedoc Pézenas

My first visit to the beautiful town of Pézenas was over 20 years ago and it left a lasting impression on me. It's an architectural gem and a place I will never tire of exploring. The old town is brimming with historical buildings and is rich with 'hôtels particuliers', period mansions adorned with wrought iron balconies and ornate doorways. I love to peer round some of the doorways or step inside the inner courtyards and admire the contents such as the magnificent renaissance staircase in Hôtel de Lacoste.

You feel immersed in history as you wander these streets and gaze at the buildings, and indeed you are. Pézenas became part of the royal estate in 1261, which brought wealth and fame to the town and furthered the fortunes of the townsfolk. The playwright Molière first visited the town in 1647 with his 'Illustrious Theatre' and again in 1653 where he found favour with the governor, the Prince of Conti, and the town makes much of this connection. The maze of medieval streets was home to many craftsmen and artisans favoured by the dukes and princes who lived here in the 15th and 16th centuries, and not a lot has changed. It's a bustling, vibrant town, a place to explore or sit and enjoy a coffee or wander the stalls at the colourful Saturday market.

The vineyards of the Pézenas appellation form a small triangle just north of the town with the river Hérault forming the eastern edge and the vines sheltered by the mountains to the north. Altitudes vary from just 20 metres close to the plain up to 300 metres in the north. The hot summers and mild winters reflect a typical Mediterranean climate, as does the low rainfall. The soil types are varied and the landscape contains some ancient volcanoes and lava flows.

It's a young appellation for red wine only, formed in 2007, and it would seem by the strict rules drawn up that they are aiming high, determined to establish a reputation for top-quality wines. For instance the yields are set low but even so most producers come in below these. There is also an uncommon ageing requirement; the vines must be at least seven years old and the wines must have a minimum of one year's ageing before they can be sold.

The landscape is garrigue-clad, mound-shaped hills bearing jagged teeth of rock jutting skywards. Sitting in the folds and creases of this rolling landscape are many pretty villages such as medieval Neffiès, Caux, Roubia and Gabian, each populated with many excellent wine makers well worth seeking out.

AOP Languedoc Pézenas

This appellation is for red wine only grown on varied soil types including limestone, schist and some volcanic basalt. It is a blend of Syrah, Grenache and Mourvèdre and a smaller amount of Carignan and Cinsault is allowed.

AOP Languedoc Cabrières

From the Pézenas vineyards it's just a hop, skip and a jump to reach the Cabrières appellation, which is just north of Pézenas and close to the Cévennes Mountains. It was once a place full of sheep and goats but they are long gone and the schist soils are now nourishing either garrigue or vines. White wine is not part of the appellation and the reds do not have the depth of character that neighbouring Faugères wines have and are best drank young. This appellation is best known for its rosé which is made using mainly Cinsault and are some of the most delicious wines of this style I have tasted.

AOP Languedoc Cabrières

This appellation is for red and rosé wine grown on schist soils. It is a blend of Syrah, Grenache and Mourvèdre and a smaller amount of Carignan and Cinsault is allowed. For the rosé white grapes can be fermented with the red varieties mentioned above. The permitted whites are Bourboulenc, Grenache Blanc, Clairette and Terret.

The remaining appellations in the eastern section of Languedoc are not allied to AOP Languedoc and are appellations in their own right, and in 2013 AOP La Clape joined their ranks.

AOP Clairette du Languedoc

Clairette is an ancient grape probably planted by the Romans. This appellation is one of the first to be established in Languedoc back in 1948 and is one of the tiniest. Clairette is a white wine, not very well known and made in small quantities mainly around the village of Adissan close to Pézenas. The wines can be made in many different styles, sometimes sweet or even fortified but more often these days they are dry with enticing flavours of honey, tropical fruit and sometimes with biscuit notes.

AOP Clairette du Languedoc

This is an appellation for white wine only grown on limestone with some quartz and schist in the north of the appellation. It is made from 100% Clairette.

AOP La Clape

La Clape probably gets its name from the Occitan word 'clapas' meaning pile of stones. In Roman times La Clape was an island but with the silting up of Narbonne port it became part of the mainland. It is a beautiful rocky and barren area dominated by the Massif de la Clape, a limestone outcrop sitting between the ancient Roman city of Narbonne and the Mediterranean Sea. The garrigue-covered rocky surface is scented with wild fennel, thyme and rosemary and deep below the surface are underground streams and many deep chasms and caves. Etched into the landscape are the parcels of vines, many of them clinging to the rocky slopes that tumble towards the deep blue water of the Mediterranean Sea. Vines have been grown here since the Roman occupation and the wines were well thought of then; however it's only in recent times that they have become highly favoured again.

The area is dotted with many villages; some are inland wine communes and others fishermen's villages now enjoyed by holiday makers. The circular village of Gruissan is a fishing village set between the étangs and the sea and crowned with a 13th-century tower built to guard the approaches to Narbonne.

Salt

In Gruissan you will find the Ile Saint Martin salt pans on the étang de l'Ayrolle. The history of salt making goes back more than a century before Christ and here in Gruissan they have been making it for many hundreds of years. Modern production began in 1911 when a Danish woman aided by a local French architect designed the salt pans. They span 250 hectares and since 1970 have provided a living for over 30 families.

Water is taken from the Mediterranean to the pans and over the ensuing weeks it moves over 40 kilometres around the pans via a network of canals and locks. During this period it is exposed to the wind, sun and rain and gradually the water is reduced through evaporation and water channelling. As this drying process occurs the layers of crystallised salt are revealed with thickness levels between 4 and 7 cm. It is now ready to be harvested.

There are various salt textures produced, moist crystals or delicate flakes. Fleur de Sel is the premium salt and literally translated means Flower of Salt. It is harvested only once a year from the very top of the salt pans and is therefore the first to be harvested.

The vines are grown on some of the stoniest land in Languedoc and are battered by the winds and sea breezes that blow nearly 300 days of the year along this coastline. And it's hot, with over 2,500 sunshine hours each year and rainfall below 20 inches. It's quite a harsh place to grow vines, but the old adage seems to apply: stressed vines produce wonderful wine. For these are some of the finest wines produced in Languedoc, perhaps aided by the tough conditions that keep the yields naturally low.

The reds have a silky texture and are infused with the fragrance of garrigue and the wild flowers that smother the rocks. There is a scientific reason for the herby flavours in the wine; it's not just imagination! The garrigue is made up of many resinous plants such as rosemary and pine, and during the hot summer days the resin evaporates into the air and is attracted to the waxy surface of the grapes where it sticks and remains and becomes part of the fermentation.

Alcohol levels tend to be high due to the grapes desiccating on the vine because of the wind and drought, but the wines tend to have good minerality and acid levels which make them fresh and enjoyable.

The whites are some of my favourites. They are full of personality and charm and are quite individual, mainly due to the use of the Bourboulenc grape variety often included in the blend. This is an ancient grape that nearly died out and was saved by the efforts of the La Clape producers and the insistence on its use in the AOP; from 2013 at least 40% of the vineyard must be planted with this delicious grape. The flavours are often highly complex with characteristics of honey, flowers, almond and tropical fruit wrapped in a fresh minerality and creamy, oaky flavours.

Up until the 2013 vintage, La Clape was part of AOP Languedoc; many people are delighted to see that its superiority and individual character have at last been recognised.

AOP La Clape

This appellation is for red and white wine grown predominantly on limestone with some sandstone and red iron-rich soils. The reds are a blend of Grenache, Syrah and Mourvèdre plus a smaller amount of Carignan and Cinsault if desired. The white wine is a blend and can contain any of the following; Bourboulenc, Clairette, Grenache Blanc, Marsanne, Roussanne, Picpoul, Vermentino (Rolle), Carignan Blanc, Terret and Ugni Blanc.

AOP Faugères

If there is one word that sums up **AOP Faugères**, it's 'schist'. The entire appellation is based on this metamorphic soil type which is a very crumbly, flaky rock. The name comes from the Greek 'skhistos', meaning something that can be split and is divisible. It's one of the oldest soils on earth. It's a metamorphic rock, so called because it was formed from clay and mud that was put under high pressure and high temperatures which initially changed it into shale and slate and then later into schist.

The colours of the schist in Faugères are numerous, ranging from yellow, ochre and orange to pale grey, and deep down in the earth a beautiful blue is sometimes found. It covers the entire area and is used for all sorts of things such as building houses, roofs and walls; I have even seen pavements made from it. The rock is foliated like a book with the leaves divided by fissures that slowly channel and trap rainwater. The vines' roots can penetrate the rock through the fissures in search of the trapped moisture.

The soils also have a thermal power. They heat up during the day and radiate the warmth to the vine long after the sun has gone down, and so the local saying might be true: 'the grapes ripen at night'.

Schist is a highly regarded soil type amongst wine makers, for it produces red wines with good natural acidity and fine tannins even when the wines are young. This vineyard area is possibly the most promising in the Languedoc, containing some very old vines and a unique terroir which has attracted many new wine makers. Amongst all the producers, new and old, there is a deep feeling of unity with everyone working towards the same goal: wine of great quality.

The majority of the vineyards are planted at relatively high altitudes in the foothills of the Cévennes Mountains north of Béziers. It's a small appellation encompassing just seven villages, each with its own personality.

Autignac is a peaceful wine-growers' village, in the most southerly part of the appellation overlooking the Béziers plain. It's a small and compact little village and many of the houses have the rounded lintel that made it easier to install the wooden foudre (large wooden barrels) and casks in which the wine was made.

Laurens is a small town with a little over 1,000 inhabitants. It's a wonderful area for flora, particularly the laurel which blooms happily here. In fact the Romans christened the town after this plant, calling it 'city of the laurel'. The 12th-century castle with its green-tiled turret sits atop the mound with the ancient houses of the old town clustered peacefully around it. The castle is now the Marie (town hall) and next to it is the bell tower once used as a watchtower in less peaceful times.

Roquessels is a tiny hamlet built at the foot of a steep rocky outcrop where the ruins of a 10th-century castle and its chapel gaze out over the valley of vines. If you climb up there you are rewarded with some fabulous views and also a plaque that describes the fascinating geology of this area.

Fos is probably the prettiest of the Faugères villages. It's very well cared for and the famous schist is everywhere, including the handsome walls and houses that are made from it. Unexpectedly the castle and the church are at the bottom of a steep lane and fanning out from here are tiny rues waiting to be explored. The surrounding vineyards are the highest in this appellation at 450 m and the hilly landscape is covered in a mixture of holm oak forest and fields of vines.

When strolling around the little town of **Faugères** with its tangled maze of narrow streets it's obvious that this was once a town of great importance. There are vestiges of the castle that once stood here and some ancient buildings with their extraordinary Saracen vaults and beautifully carved stone lintels. In the hills behind the town there are three 16th-century windmills and leading to and from them are pathways which pass by a number of capitelles or carabelles as they are often called here.

Caussiniojouls means 'limestone plateau in the clouds' and at 315 m this beautiful and peaceful village deserves this lovely name. The castle in the centre of the village dates back to the 10th century and indeed stepping into this village is like stepping back in time. It's set amongst some of the most beautiful landscape in Faugères and the vineyards are in the hands of some of the most talented wine makers too.

Cabrerolles makes up the seventh of the Faugères villages and along with the hamlets of La Liquière, Lenthéric, Aigues-Vives and La Borie Nouvelle is home to some of the brightest stars in Faugères wine making.

If you approach the appellation from the Béziers plain you are very conscious of the rise in altitude and the vines growing on the schist soils reward you with a delicious freshness and minerality. Most of the vineyards have a southerly aspect although some winemakers have looked for north-facing slopes in order to slow the alcoholic ripening so that it occurs at the same time as phenolic maturity.

This is predominantly a country of red wine made from a blend of typical Mediterranean grape varieties. The resulting wines are a cross between a southern Rhône and a more rustic Corbières. It took a long time for the white wines of Faugères to be accepted into the AOP but eventually in 2005 they were awarded appellation status. Grenache Blanc, Roussanne and Marsanne are usually the major grapes in the blend and a little splash of Vermentino adds a delightful citrus note. The wines are often crisp with mineral overtones and an intriguing personality and have been well worth the wait.

AOP Faugères

This appellation is for red, rosé and white wine grown exclusively on schist soils. The red and rosé is a blend of Syrah, Grenache, Mourvèdre, Carignan and Cinsault. The white wine blend can contain Grenache Blanc, Roussanne, Marsanne, Vermentino, Bourboulenc and Clairette.

Fine de Faugères

Fine de Faugères is an eau de vie (French brandy similar to Cognac or Armagnac). It was the first eau de vie to be regulated in the Languedoc region and most importantly, the only one to be distilled using the same type of still as used in Cognac, called an alambic.

It was awarded its appellation in 1948 but had been made in the region since 1852. It ceased production some 30 years ago but recommenced in 2000.

It is distilled from the fine residue of wine made of grapes grown in the Faugères appellation (Grenache, Syrah, Carignan, Mourvèdre etc.), and the distillation takes place in the February following the harvest. There is only one distiller and he collects the wine from the producers and distils it for them. The brandy must mature at least five years in barrel and before bottling is broken down with local water from Mont Roucou to bring it to 30% ABV. It has a pleasant character, sweet and elegant, quite fruity, soft and smooth.

AOP Saint-Chinian

The town of Saint-Chinian gets its name from a 9th-century monk called Anian who settled here and worked tirelessly to clear the area and plant the vines. He was canonised in the 11th century and the region got its name due to the way the word 'saint' is pronounced in the local language, which is 'sainch'. Today the little town of Saint-Chinian is a lively market town with people thronging to its main square on Thursdays and Sundays for one of the best markets in Languedoc.

Like most of the Languedoc this area suffered many struggles throughout its history, especially through the wars of religion. At the time of the French Revolution the local industries of wool and tanning collapsed and shortly afterwards the area was devastated by a terrible flood. The saviour for the region was in fact phylloxera. It began its attack in the eastern part of the region and slowly marched west. By the time it reached the area around Béziers the people of Saint-Chinian knew how to protect the vineyards by planting resistant rootstocks. Many of the industrial labourers turned to viticulture and vineyard plantings increased and the resulting wine helped the nation get back on its feet.

The Saint-Chinian appellation is north-west of Béziers between the River Orb and the Vernazobre valley. The vineyard area is surrounded by the Caroux hills with the Espinouse Mountains looming up in the background. The appellation covers 20 villages scattered around the region and located in the two distinct halves, based on the soil types. Schist is in the north where the area meets the Faugères appellation and clay/limestone in the south towards the Minervois. The soils of the Saint-Chinian region are poorer than those of its more southerly counterparts and therefore yields tend to be low and the wines have a concentrated perfume of black fruit and are often deliciously spicy and herby.

Although the climate is mainly Mediterranean, there is some continental influence in the higher northerly areas where altitudes reach 400 m. The wind and the sun dominate and rainfall is very low, mainly happening in the winter months apart from the odd storm during the summer.

Carignan is not as influential here as it is in other parts of Languedoc, so it's Grenache, Syrah and Mourvèdre that share centre stage. The wines are of high quality and will vary quite considerably depending where they were grown. Wines grown on the arid schist soils in the north at altitudes above 200 m are often quite sharply etched with a delicate bouquet and interesting minerality with refreshing acidity. The tannins soften early and the wine is often silky smooth within a few years of the vintage.

The wines produced in the southern area around the town of Saint-Chinian are grown at around 100 m. The clay limestone soils found here produce softer, rounder wines with flavours of blackcurrants, raspberries and cherries. They have a wonderful deep colour and are often age-worthy.

The red wines of Saint-Chinian have been highly regarded since the late 1800s, so much so that patients in some Parisian hospitals were prescribed them to aid their recovery!

The white wines must be a blend of at least two grapes and Grenache Blanc must account for 30% of the blend accompanied by Marsanne, Roussanne or Vermentino. The addition of Vermentino adds a zing of lime and grapefruit flavours which gives the wine freshness, something that white wines from hot climates can lack. The wine maker can also choose to add a small percentage of Viognier, Clairette, Carignan Blanc, Bourboulenc or Macabeu if he wishes and wines are often barrel-fermented and/or matured to add complexity and structure. The wines often have aromas of fresh citrus, apricots and nuts with soft spices and when grown on the schist soils they will have notes of mineral and aniseed.

AOP Saint-Chinian

This appellation is for red, rosé and white wine. In the north of the district the vines are grown on schist soils and in the south clay/limestone. The red and rosé is a blend and can contain Grenache, Syrah, Lladoner Pelut, Carignan and Cinsault. For the white wine, 90% of the blend must be selected from Grenache Blanc, Marsanne, Roussanne and Vermentino and the balance from Carignan Blanc, Clairette, Viognier, Macabeu and Bourboulenc.

The Saint-Chinian Crus

Appellations are mainly based on soil types and due to geological forces many millions of years ago the Languedoc-Roussillon soils are quite a mixture. Some of the appellations cover very large areas of land containing different soil types and the wines can vary enormously from one end of the appellation to the other. The authorities recognise this and over the coming years more and more appellations will be created from within large AOPs and referred to as 'cru'. So far Languedoc has four 'cru' appellations and two are found in the north of the Saint-Chinian region, **Berlou** to the west and **Roquebrun** to the east.

AOP Saint-Chinian Berlou

The road that winds its way to Berlou from the town of Saint-Chinian takes you closer to the dramatic Caroux hills and Espinouse Mountains beyond. The appellation is spread over five villages: Berlou, Cessenon-sur-Orb, Prades-sur-Vernazobre, Roquebrun and Vieussan, and the vineyards are planted at altitudes between 150 and 400 m.

All the villages are very beautiful but I especially like Vieussan, which has a wonderful old stone bridge with an exceptionally broad span over the River Orb. The village houses appear to be built on top of one another, clinging to the rocks and protected by an ancient tower that looms above them.

The little village of Berlou has a population of 200 and even though there are only eight pupils the school is still open for business. The village co-operative is the main producer of Cru Berlou and there are only about four or five independent producers. It's a well-run co-operative with only 12 growers contracted and each of them takes their turn to man the tasting room which is open every day including Sundays. Opposite the tasting room is a wonderful restaurant, Le Faitout – a hidden gem.

Berlou received its appellation for red wine only in 2005 and producers must adhere to stricter regulations than AOP Saint-Chinian requires. These include hand harvesting and lower yields than the rest of Saint-Chinian, and the wine must be aged for a minimum of 15 months before it can be released for sale. This means it cannot be sold until December 1st of the year following the harvest.

All the vineyards are southerly-facing on extremely steep slopes and are planted in eight different terroirs within the Berlou appellation, a place where wolves once roamed. Carignan is more important here than in the neighbouring Cru Roquebrun and must make up a minimum of 30% of the blend with Grenache, Syrah and Mourvèdre each accounting for a minimum of 20%, and all the vines must be at least ten years old.

Typically the wines have black fruit flavours, liquorice and grilled and roasted notes with silky tannins of great finesse.

AOP Saint-Chinian Berlou

This cru appellation is for red wine only grown on schist and sandstone soils. It is a blend of Grenache, Syrah, Mourvèdre and Carignan which are grown at a slightly lower yield than AOP St Chinian.

AOP Saint-Chinian Roquebrun

The village of Roquebrun stands on a mountainside below its Carolingian tower and over-looking a bend in the beautiful River Orb. The river bursts into life in the Upper Languedoc Nature Park and winds its way through many villages on its way to meet the sea at Valras. At Vieussan and Roquebrun its refreshing aquamarine-coloured mountain waters are popular with kayakers and bathers during the summer months. Roquebrun is a small village with a distinctly Mediterranean feel and a microclimate that has earned it the nickname 'Nice of Hérault'. Mimosa, orange and lemon trees thrive here, as do the famous Mediterranean Gardens with over 400 species of medicinal and aromatic plants.

Roquebrun

Although this appellation encompasses fewer villages than Berlou, four rather than five, it is the larger of the two in terms of hectares planted and the vineyards are situated at a slightly lower altitude with the maximum being 350 m. Its production is almost double that of Berlou with the highly regarded co-operative **Cave les vins de Roquebrun** being the majority producer. The co-operative is based in Roquebrun and the other villages in the appellation are Cessenon-sur-Orb, Saint-Nazaire-de-Ladarez and Vieussan.

The maturation period is the same as Berlou with the wine only released for sale after December 1st of the year following the harvest. The blend is usually dominated by Grenache and Syrah and the blending regulations are head scratchingly intricate! However you are rewarded with mighty, commanding wines that are complex and generous, spicy and supple and the perfect match for a hearty dinner.

AOP Saint-Chinian Roquebrun

This cru appellation is for red wine only grown exclusively on schist soils. It is a blend with quite complex criteria: Syrah, Grenache and Mourvèdre must represent at least 70% of the blend and Carignan and Mourvèdre less than 20%. Grenache has to represent more than 20% and Syrah at least 25%. Cinsault is not allowed.

Olives

Olive production was of great importance in the Languedoc-Roussillon long before the vine became so dominant and cultivation goes back to the Roman occupation. In 1956 Languedoc-Roussillon suffered an extreme winter with very low temperatures that resulted in the death of many of the olive trees. Now with the government encouraging farmers to diversify many more olive trees are being planted again, adding to the beauty of the landscape.

There are over 300 varieties of olive found along the Mediterranean coastline of Italy, France and Spain and two of the most popular in Languedoc-Roussillon are Luque and Picholine.

Luque is often referred to as the Rolls-Royce of olives. It does not give a lot of oil and you need twice as many Luque olives as other varieties to make a litre of oil. They are wonderful eating olives, fruity, crunchy and salty and delicious with a glass of Muscat.

In the 17th century two Italian brothers called the Picholinis discovered how to make the olive edible and still keep its green colour. The method was applied to the olives in the Languedoc, which then took the name of the inventors. The Picholine olive is very fruity, green, crisp and peppery.

CHAPTER 6

Western Languedoc

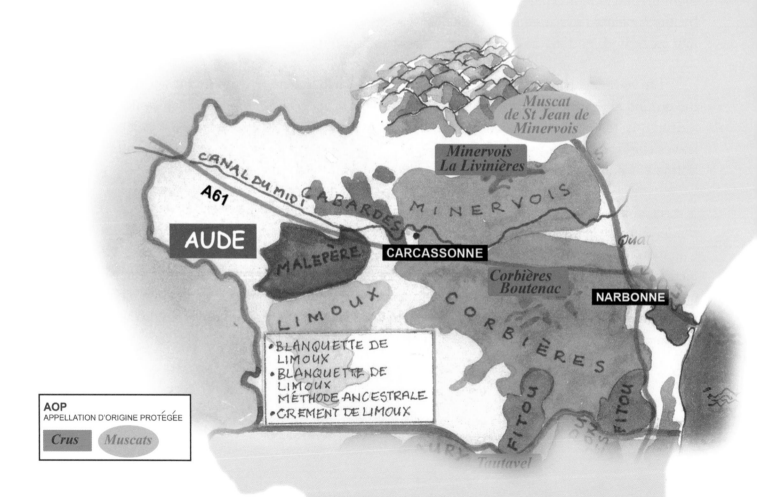

AOP
APPELLATION D'ORIGINE PROTÉGÉE

Crus   Muscats

AOP Minervois

I live in the Minervois and whenever I have been away my heart leaps when I return to this beautiful place. I head north out of Carcassonne and drive towards the Black Mountains, then turn eastwards and skirt the foot of the hills and enter the part of Languedoc that has become my home. The layers of steep hills look black with the pine forest plantations which have given them the name Montagne Noire and at the foot of them the vineyards begin. In the winter their beauty is painted russet and brown and as the spring begins the awakening of the vines brings tiny green buds and the trees dotting the landscape sport delicate white and pink blossom.

The summers here are hot and the land is often parched but the vines find water deep in the ground and their lush green foliage keeps the land looking alive and flourishing, which indeed it is, for as autumn arrives we bring in the harvest. The vines are heavy with fruit as the leaves start to turn and by mid-October the landscape has completely changed colour and has donned its autumn attire of bright scarlet, dazzling gold and rich orange.

The Minervois is mainly in the department of the Aude with some of it straddling the border into the Hérault. It stretches from Carcassonne to Narbonne and northwards from the Canal du Midi towards the Montagne Noire. It's a place of fantastic beauty and with an incredible history. At its heart is the village of Minerve which 800 years ago sheltered a small group of Cathars from the Pope's mercenary Simon de Montfort. The siege ended in a bloody massacre and the lives of the people are remembered with a stone-carved dove beside the village church.

As you pass through the Minervois you will notice the changing landscape from one end to the other, so it's no surprise to learn that the Minervois contains a number of different terroirs and, although there are no signs to tell you when you have passed from one to another, they have names.

Le Petit Causse is in the north of the Minervois and has a very Mediterranean climate with low rainfall and hot, dry conditions. The limestone soils are covered in garrigue and it's a wonderful place to walk as each step you take will release intoxicating scents of lavender, sage, rosemary and wild thyme. It is home to the beautiful village of Minerve, built on a limestone rock that is almost an island carved out of the landscape by the rivers Brian and Cesse. The two rivers meet at the foot of the village in a deep gorge and the waters continue to flow southwards by one name, La Cesse.

The white limestone is barely covered by the shallow soils and it's hard to believe that the south-facing vines that cling to the hillsides can survive without irrigation. But deep below the surface the limestone has been hollowed out by rivers, streams and rainwater and the vines can send their roots several metres in search of a drink. Along the way they pick up the minerals in the soil, which are often reflected in the flavours of the wine.

Les Serres is the eastern section and includes the Serre d'Oupia and the Pech de Bize which are some of the driest parts of Minervois, a place where there is often great water stress. The river Cesse flows through this area and looks worryingly empty as it goes underground in summer months. The soils are limestone and full of pebbles and the heat and drought often suit Mourvèdre, which produces silky, sleek, spicy red wines.

Minerve

The Terraces and Piedmont is the area that extends northwards from the River Aude in wide terraces and gentle slopes known as Balcons de l'Aude. All the slopes and terraces face east or south and get maximum exposure to the sun, and some are sitting alongside the two major rivers, the Argent Double and the Ognon. There are a lot of rocky ridges in the eastern section and the steeply sloping vineyards here are bordered by garrigue, whilst other parts of this area are mellow with gently sloping hillsides and flatter fields where casots (wine-growers' stone huts) stand at regular intervals and capitelles huddle up against the crumbling enclosing walls.

La Clamoux takes its name from the river that winds through this south-westerly part of the Minervois and this section is protected from the Mediterranean influences by a series of hills. The winters are mild and the growing season is long and the fruit have time to build flavours.

Les Côtes Noires, as the name suggests, are the slopes below the Montagne Noire; they all face south, giving a perfect aspect for grape growing. The most easterly side will feel some of the Atlantic influences that neighbouring Cabardès enjoys but the dry weather in late summer and early autumn helps with ripening and harvesting. The soil can be quite shallow and relatively poor but this can help to control the vines' vigour and yields tend to be reasonably low.

In 2012 94% of AOP Minervois wine was red, 4% rosé and only a minuscule 2% was white. This is quite normal for traditional-style wines made in a climate that is much more suited to producing red wines with body and high alcohol. However, if the wine maker seeks out cooler growing areas and plants white varieties that can flourish in the heat and drought, some good examples can be made. They will never taste like a white wine from northern France such as Sancerre or Chablis, but the richness of these wines will suit the Mediterranean foods much better.

The red wines are variable, making it difficult to describe a typical Minervois, and this may be due to the differing terroir across the district. However Syrah is well loved in the Minervois and many of the wines contain a large percentage of this grape. Syrah can offer delicious flavours of blackberry and damsons with a hint of black pepper and spice from the cooler areas, but unfortunately some can be rather jammy from the hotter spots.

AOP Minervois

This appellation is for red, rosé and white wine although red represents the vast majority of production. The grapes are grown on a mixture of soils including clay, limestone, sandstone, marble and schist. The red and rosé is a blend of Syrah, Grenache, Mourvèdre plus smaller amounts of Carignan, Cinsault, Terret, Aspiran and Picpoul Noir are permitted. The white blend can include Marsanne, Roussanne, Macabeu, Bourboulenc, Grenache Blanc, Vermentino and Muscat Blanc à Petits Grains.

AOP Minervois La Livinière

The area around the village of La Livinière has been inhabited by man for several millennia. The Romans were here in force and many villas were built by retired centurions. There is archaeological evidence that wine was produced in La Livinière by the Romans; indeed the area is said to take its name from 'cella vinaria', Latin for 'wine cellar'. The village of La Livinière is ancient and beautiful with its extremely narrow streets and stone-built houses and is well worth a visit. The church is particularly lovely and the tower is unusually crowned with a dome, said to be an idea brought back from Bethlehem by the crusaders. This landmark is the symbol of the cru quality and sits proudly on the label of the La Livinière wines.

You can pick up a leaflet outlining a walk around the village of La Livinière from the tourist office in Minerve, where they have a great many others too. The walk takes you through the terroir surrounding the village where you will see tiny parcels of vines clinging to the stony ground, many of them enclosed by ancient walls and surrounded by garrigue. Some of the vines are planted on steep slopes and are staked to the ground to protect them from the mighty Tramontane when it blows. You will come across some ancient wells and a great many capitelles of all shapes and sizes. As well as vines you will see olive groves, some old and some planted recently; their beautiful silvery leaves sway in the ever-present breeze. There is even a Roman olive oil press found along one of the winding lanes that criss-cross this beautiful landscape.

In 1999 the first cru of the Languedoc-Roussillon was created. The terroir lies in the foothills of the Montagne Noire within Le Petit Causse and encompasses the villages of Azillanet, Félines-Minervois, Siran, Cesseras, Azille and La Livinière, this last giving its name to the appellation. For a Minervois wine to qualify for cru status it must be grown within the delimited

La Livinière

boundaries which are based on terroir and the vines must be grown at lower yields than other Minervois wines. The soils in this area are stony and include limestone and marl, and the vines are planted at cooling altitudes where there is a considerable drop in night-time temperature that slows ripening, allowing the gradual build of flavours, and also maintains freshness. The result is wines that are perfumed and have higher acidity and firmer tannins, giving the structure needed to age wine for extended periods.

It's an appellation for red wine only and Syrah often plays a starring role; however, the wine must have at least two of the authorised grapes and be aged in barrel or tank for at least 15 months. The wines display intense 'garrigue' perfume and concentrated black fruits, and often have a distinct black olive tapenade character and notes of pepper and spice summoning up the warmth of the Mediterranean sunshine in every sip.

AOP Minervois La Livinière

This cru appellation was the first in Languedoc and is for red wine only grown on limestone and marl soils at slightly lower yield than AOP Minervois. It is a blend of at least 2 from Syrah, Mourvèdre, Grenache and Carignan and if desired a small amount of Carignan, Cinsault, Terret Noir, Aspiran and Picpoul Noir can be included. The wine must be aged in barrel or tank for at least 15 months before bottling and being released for sale.

AOP Cabardès

The region of Cabardès is just 10 km north-west of Carcassonne, encompassing 18 villages and bordering the Minervois to the east. It is named after the Lords of Cabaret who defended Châteaux de Lastours against Simon de Montfort during the Cathar Crusade of 1209.

Although this is only a small appellation of about 550 hectares, the landscape varies considerably from one side of the district to the other. The area closest to Carcassonne has gently sloping hills and altitude reaches a maximum of 100 m. This part of Cabardès resembles the western part of the Minervois which it borders. In the heart of the appellation, around the very pretty village of Aragon, the landscape alters considerably. It becomes rugged and mountainous and altitudes reach 350 m as you draw closer to the Montagne Noire.

Despite the medieval links this appellation is one of the youngest in France, having only become official in February 1999. It stands out from the rest of the Languedoc because of the grape varieties planted here, which are an equal split between Mediterranean and Atlantic (Bordeaux) varieties. The choice of planting is mainly due to the winds that blow here. There is the humid Mediterranean wind named the Cers which blows from the east and the wind known as the Marin which is cooler and comes from the direction of the Atlantic to the west.

These conditions coupled with the mix of soil types and the varying altitudes create a number of terroirs, each demanding very different grape types. The cooler conditions found in the western part of the region are ideal for the Atlantic varieties. So here the majority of plantings are Cabernet Sauvignon, Merlot, Cabernet Franc, Cot (also known as Malbec/Auxerrois) and a grape you may not have come across before: Fer Servadou. The hotter eastern side is more suited to the Mediterranean grapes, Syrah and Grenache.

Cabardès is an appellation for red and rosé wine only and those producers making a white wine are labelling it as IGP or possibly Vin du France. The mixture of grape varieties and terroirs enables the wine maker to obtain rich, complex and well balanced wines. The lively, expressive, ripe fruit of the Atlantic varieties blend perfectly with the soft, rich aromas and dark, full-bodied Mediterranean grapes. Cabardès wines are generally dark and complex with rich developing aromas of blackcurrant, black cherries, ripe prunes and violets. Their ageing potential stretches from two to ten years. The rosé wines are hard to find and only 10% of the production is made this way. When you do find a bottle you will be rewarded with a beautifully perfumed nose and refreshing red fruit flavours of cherry and raspberry.

AOP Cabardès

This appellation is for red and rosé although only 10% is pink. The vines are grown on limestone with granite and gneiss and on the higher slopes there is also some schist soils in parts. The wines must be an equal split between Atlantic and Mediterranean varieties using Merlot, Cabernet Sauvignon, Cabernet Franc, Syrah, Grenache, Cot (Malbec), Fer Servadou and Cinsault.

AOP Côtes de Malepère

Although the Malepère district claims a great history of wine making it was only in the 1970s that VDQS status was granted. This is an intermediary wine designation and is a testing ground for would-be AOCs to prove that wines from all the producers share a common personality before they can be awarded full AOC status. It took a long time but on May 2nd 2007 the appellation was granted.

Currently Malepère is an obscure region but it's well worth a visit and offers a very different terrain to the more recognisable Languedoc appellations. It is a hilly area south-west of the city of Carcassonne, which is included in the appellation along with 31 other towns and villages. It is the most westerly appellation of the Languedoc and although hilly is less so than other districts and more open. The land is planted with many crops and in summertime huge swathes of sunflowers can be seen cheerfully turning their heads to the sun and the vines are interwoven within the patchwork landscape.

There are many fascinating medieval circular villages to visit. They were built this way to form ramparts to protect the inhabitants. The Cathar religion was strong here and the area is immersed in history and folklore.

Atlantic grape varieties dominate the blend of this red and rosé appellation. White wine is not allowed but you will find many fine examples of Viognier, Sauvignon Blanc and Chardonnay made as IGP wines. For the reds, Merlot is the star player forming the major part of the blend with Cot, Cabernet Sauvignon, Cabernet Franc and Grenache in supporting roles and Syrah is kept in the wings, forbidden to make an appearance yet. For the rosé, Merlot is elbowed sideways and Cabernet Franc dominates the blend, and now Syrah can make its entrance.

Although the Bordeaux varieties dominate the blends, the wines bear more similarity to those from the Gascony region of south-west France than those from Bordeaux. The wines are usually deep in colour and have redcurrant, raspberry and blackcurrant on the nose, with hints of spices, truffle, pepper and a lightly wooded scent. They can be light and simple and made for early drinking, but some have a powerful, rounded palate with a tannic structure and good acid balance, and develop well when matured in casks.

AOP Côtes de Malepère

This appellation is for red and rosé wines grown on clay/limestone soils. The reds must contain a minimum of 50% Merlot and 20% each of Cot (Malbec) and Cabernet Franc plus they can also contain small amounts of Cabernet Sauvignon, Grenache and Cinsault. The rosé wines must contain a minimum 50% Cabernet Franc plus a choice of Syrah, Merlot, Cot, Cabernet Sauvignon, Grenache or Cinsault. Note, the rosé can contain Syrah but in the red it is not allowed.

The AOP Wines of Limoux

Legend has it that it was a cold winter in 1531 when the monks at the Abbey of Saint-Hilaire near Limoux were making their usual white wine. Limoux is in the foothills of the eastern Pyrenees, so the altitude coupled with the breezes coming across from the Atlantic made this an ideal area for white wine production and still does.

Limoux

But in the winter of 1531 it was so cold that the wine did not completely ferment and the monks bottled it without realising the fermentation was not over and therefore sugar and yeast were still present in the wine. The wine was kept in the cellar over winter and as the temperatures rose in the springtime the fermentation began again. The carbon dioxide produced by the yeast could not escape from the bottle and so dissolved into the wine, making it fizzy. But as the pressure rose in the bottle the yeast expired before it could convert all the sugar, leaving a sweet sparkling wine.

Legend says the monks were pleased with the wine and endeavoured to make it each year and about 150 years later news of this sparkling wine came to the ears of another monk who made his way to the abbey to find out more about it. His name was Dom Pérignon and he later returned to his abbey in the Champagne region of northern France, taking the recipe with him.

Limoux is still famous for sparkling wines and these days you can buy three types including **Blanquette Ancestral**, which is much the same as the one the monks made. It's a low-alcohol, sweet and fruity fizz, made using a local grape variety called Mauzac, and tastes a little like a high-quality cider. It's a good accompaniment to a slice of cake, or you could finish a meal with a light fruit mousse and glass of Blanquette Ancestral.

The other two sparkling wines made in Limoux are made the same way as Champagne but using local grape varieties. One of these is called **Blanquette du Limoux**, which is usually a dry wine made from the Mauzac grape plus small amounts of Chardonnay and Chenin Blanc and aged for a short time in the cellar before being released for sale. It is light and easy to drink with flavours of bruised apples and its low cost encourages people to drink it at any time.

If you're looking for something a little more like Champagne then you will like the final Limoux sparkler called **Crémant du Limoux**. It spends a longer time in the cellar and is produced using Chardonnay plus Chenin Blanc, Mauzac and, for the rosé version, Pinot Noir. Crémant du Limoux is often complex, creamy and biscuity with flavours of apricot, acacia and apple plus citrus notes of tangerine and grapefruit. It is a superb rival for Champagne and usually the price is much lower.

What's the difference between Blanquette and Crémant?

The grape mix – *Blanquette must contain a minimum of 90% Mauzac and maximum 10% Chardonnay and Chenin Blanc. The same grapes are used to make Crémant but Chardonnay is the dominant grape.*

Ageing – *Blanquette ages on its lees for a minimum of 9 months and Crémant for a minimum of 15 months.*

Giving its name to the region is the pretty market town of Limoux with its handsome church and interesting Friday market which takes place in the pretty central square called Place de la République.

It is in this square that a fascinating event takes place every year. The ancient carnival of Limoux is said to be the longest in Europe, starting in January and ending the Sunday before Palm Sunday. It harks back to medieval times and involves the election of a King which is in fact a straw doll. The people taking part in the carnival dress in beautiful Pierrot costumes and masks, and each weekend they parade around the main square waving their wands and following a noisy group of musicians. On the final night the King is tried and although strongly defended he is always found guilty and always burned in the centre of the square. The Pierrots watch the proceedings and throw their wands into the fire, calling out the phrase, 'Goodbye, poor Carnival; you go, and I remain until next year.'

The town is 25 km south of Carcassonne and lies on the River Aude, which flows through the town from north to south; there are a number of interesting bridges connecting the east and west halves. The town is at the centre of the Limoux wine region which backs onto the Pyrenees and runs along the upper valley of the Aude. It is a comfortable place in which to live as it is noticeably cooler and is sheltered by natural barriers that produce a split between an Atlantic and Mediterranean climate.

The region is divided into four different terroirs based on the influence of the different climates found in each one. **Terroir Meditérranéen** is the most easterly of the four areas and nudges up to the Corbières. Of the 4 terroir this one has the lowest altitude and the warmest climate and the wines are rich and fruity. **Terroir d'Autan** is named after the hot wind of the area and is in the heart of the region, surrounding the town of Limoux. There is slightly more elevation here, but even so the wines can lack freshness, but all the same but they are deliciously fruity. **Terroir Océanique** is found in the most westerly part of the region where the Atlantic influences are at their highest. The wines from here are some of my favourites perhaps due to the relatively cool climate and are fresh and fairly delicate with great finesse. Terroir Haute Valleé is the most southerly of the terroirs and the one lying closest to the Pyrenees. The vines are planted at lofty heights of up to 500 m and these cool situations are ideal for growing Chardonnay which produces elegant wines with freshness and often quite nervy acidity.

Although the majority of wine from Limoux is sparkling there are some excellent still wines made here in the four terroirs. The first of these to receive appellation status in 1993 was **AOP Limoux Blanc**, which can be made from the local grape Mauzac as well as Chardonnay and Chenin Blanc. Although the wines can be made from just one of these grapes or a blend, the rule is that the vineyard must be planted with at least 15% of Mauzac! The rules for these wines are indeed strict and sometimes bizarre. For instance there is a rule that limits the size of the harvesting trailer to a maximum of 3,000 kg!

AOP Limoux Rouge was introduced in 2004 and although the rules are less strict they are quite rigorously defined. Sadly this has not led to consistency and I think the authorities missed an opportunity by insisting the wine should be made mainly with Merlot when Pinot Noir might have been a better choice. Pinot Noir is planted here but much of it is destined for Crémant production or IGP wines and is not allowed in Limoux Rouge.

The Traditional Method

The traditional method to make sparkling wine is exactly the same as the method used to make Champagne. You begin by making a base wine in the normal way. Following blending the wine is bottled and the **Liqueur de Tirage** is added, which is sugar and yeast. The bottles are closed with a crown cap, much like a beer cap, and put into a cool cellar where the yeast slowly gets to work on the added sugar and gradually the second fermentation takes place. This produces about 1 to 2% alcohol and CO_2 which dissolves into the wine, making it fizzy.

Once all the sugar has been devoured the yeast dies and the bottle now contains the dead yeast cells known as **lees**. The bottle stays in the cellar for the regulated amount of time during which the lees break down (**autolysis**) and produce a much-desired rich, creamy character. The longer the lees stay in the bottle, the more of this autolytic character will form.

When the wine has finished maturing the bottles are put into a rack called a **gyropalette**, although some are still done by hand in a **pupitre**. The bottles enter this process horizontally and each day they are gently shaken and the angle turned (**remuage**) until eventually the bottles are vertical, pointing downwards, and the lees have gathered in the neck of the bottle.

Next, the neck of the bottle is frozen by passing it through frozen brine solution and now it is safe to turn the bottle the correct way up as the frozen lees will not disperse. The next step is to remove the crown cap and the pressure in the bottle shoots the frozen plug of sediment out of the bottle. This process is called **disgorgement**.

Now it's time for the dosage, which is a process to top up the bottle and add sweetness if it's required. In Champagne the wines have sugar added at this stage but in Limoux the dosage is usually just wine.

Finally the bottles are closed with a cork which is held in place with a wire and covered by foil.

There are many independent producers of Limoux wines and many of them make both the sparkling and the still wines. However they are completely outnumbered by the growers in the region and therefore the two co-operative wineries, **Les Caves du Sieur d'Arques** and **Anne de Joyeuse**, are very important.

The AOPs of Limoux

The Limoux appellations are all grown on limestone plus sandstone, quartz and clay in four terroir.

AOP Blanquette de Limoux

A sparkling wine made by the traditional method using a minimum of 90% Mauzac and up to 10% Chenin Blanc and Chardonnay. It is aged for a minimum of 9 months on its lees before being disgorged and released for sale.

AOP Crémant du Limoux

A sparkling wine made by the traditional method using a minimum of 40% Chardonnay and between 20 and 40% Chenin Blanc with a maximum of 90% of both. Mauzac and Pinot Noir are allowed to complete the blend and the wine must age on its lees for a minimum of 15 months.

AOP Blanquette Ancestral

A sweet sparkling wine made using the ancestral method which involves halting the fermentation and then beginning again once bottled but finally stopping it again before all the sugar has been transformed into alcohol. Made from 100% Mauzac and aged for only 2 months on its lees, it is low in alcohol, at around 7%.

AOP Limoux Blanc

A still white wine made as a blend or a single varietal using Chardonnay, Chenin Blanc and Mauzac. The grapes must be hand harvested, fermented in barrel then matured in barrel until at least May following the vintage. Mauzac should form 15% of vineyard planting.

AOP Limoux Rouge

A red wine that must be a blend of at least three grape varieties. The blend can contain Merlot, Cot, Cabernet Sauvignon, Cabernet Franc, Grenache, Syrah and Carignan and must spend at least 7 months in tank or barrel before being bottled and released for sale.

Toques et Clochers

One of the finest producers of still and sparkling wines is **Les Caves du Sieur d'Arques**, which is a cave co-operative in the town of Limoux and is responsible for about three-quarters of the production in the area. They produce a 100% Chardonnay AOP Limoux Blanc called '**Toques et Clochers**', which is made from fruit grown in all four of the Limoux terroirs. They call this wine their 'petit Meursault'.

Toques et Clochers takes its name from the annual auction of exceptional barrels of Chardonnay produced from the best parcels of land. The auction is held in Limoux on the Sunday before Easter every year. A gala dinner is cooked by a celebrity chef (hence the Toques – the chef's traditional tall hat) whilst the proceeds of the auction go to a different Limoux wine village each year to be used for the restoration of the bell tower (the Clocher).

AOP Corbières

The Corbières is a diverse and contrasting region where cicadas sing and buzzards circle lazily against a deep blue sky, over wild, windswept garrigue. The region was formed when the Pyrenees were thrust up 500 million years ago and much of this wild and hilly region is in the crumple zone of that activity. These wrinkles have formed winding valleys, gorges and rocky plateaux that produce many different micro-climates and hundreds of different terroirs for the wine maker to experiment in.

It's the biggest appellation in the Aude department and also in Languedoc and the fourth largest in France. It produces exciting, dense and herby red and rosé wines and a small amount of increasingly well-made whites. The area is large and the terroirs so diverse that the wines are considerably different from one end of the region to the other, tending to be as varied as the terroir. Although there are 11 named terroirs, they are not official in terms of the AOP and so are of little help when selecting a wine. The basic distinction is between those grown near to the sea and those grown inland towards the mountains.

It was not that long ago that the Corbières was seen as the place that produced cheap, rough, bulk wines. It had been dominated by co-operatives that had a philosophy of quantity over quality. Over the last 15 years there has been a gradual change driven by quality conscious and mainly independent producers who have formed a united front and with determination are turning around the fortunes of this huge wine district.

Carignan and Grenache are the most important grapes here and often dominate the red wine blends although Syrah and Mourvèdre have settled in well after being introduced over 30 years ago. The wines still tend to be full bodied, rugged and hearty and without the elegance that I associate with Minervois wines. They are the perfect foil for wild boar stew or other equally robust dishes. Rosé and white are also allowed in the appellation but make up a small percentage of the total production. The whites are often a well-made blend of Macabeu, Grenache Blanc, Marsanne and Rousanne sometimes fermented or matured in oak to add complexity but often just fresh and fruity and made for early consumption.

Lagrasse

AOP Corbières

This appellation is for red, rosé and white wines although red makes up 95% of production. The Corbières is the largest appellation in Languedoc and the soils are chiefly limestone plus schist, red clay, galets roulés and marl. Carignan is the dominant grape for red wines plus Grenache, Mourvèdre, Syrah, Lladoner Pelut and a small amount of Cinsault. The same grapes can be used to make rosé but more Cinsault is allowed, up to 70%. The white wine is a blend of Grenache Blanc, Bourboulenc, Marsanne, Roussanne, Vermentino, Clairette, Terret and up to 10% Muscat.

There are many pretty villages in the Corbières and it's a perfect place for exploring. I like the exceptionally long row of plane trees as you approach or leave the little village of Tournissan, and the fascinating lavoir in Talairan that has different areas for soaping and rinsing when washing your clothes, and I often visit the village of Ribaute to go swimming in the river Orbieu on a hot day. This river also flows through the beautiful village of Lagrasse, which was once the capital of the Corbières and an important wine village due to the abbey of Saint-Marie d'Orbieu, founded by Charlemagne in 799. The Saturday market takes place in the ancient covered market which is surrounded by 14th to 16th-century houses, many with interesting carving along the arcade.

AOP Corbières Boutenac

This is the only Corbières cru and along with the two Saint-Chinian crus followed in the footsteps of Minervois-La Livinière, which was the first cru in Languedoc. The small appellation covers ten villages around the village of Boutenac. The landscape comprises broad fields of vines bounded by low, gently rising hills dotted with tall parasol pines. The red stony soils are exposed to the warm Mediterranean sun and cooled by the fierce Tramontane wind that frequently blows here. Rainfall is low, often none falls at all during the long summer months, but the ancient Carignan vines, some of them a century old, have deep roots and can withstand the drought. Carignan is the most important grape and can make up to 50% of the blend. The wine can be aged in vat or barrel and must spend at least 11 months in bottle before being tasted and awarded Corbières Boutenac status.

This is a young appellation, only formed in 2005, and from the beginning producers have aimed high and worked in co-operation with each other to ensure that this cru is of a very high standard. Carignan is the dominant grape in the blend and the wines often have a great purity of fruit, good substance and depth of character.

AOP Corbières Boutenac

This cru appellation is for red wine only grown on clay, limestone, red iron-rich soils and stones called galets roulés. The vines have a slightly lower yield compared to Corbières and the wine must be a blend of between 30 and 50% Carignan from vines that must be at least 9 years old. The blend is completed using either Grenache, Syrah and Mourvèdre and can include all four grapes. The wine must undergo 11 months ageing before it is tasted and awarded Corbières Boutenac status.

AOP Fitou

The Fitou appellation was created in 1948, making it the oldest appellation for red wine in Languedoc. Local politics at the time caused the appellation to be delimited into two districts with standard Corbières wine grown on the land in between. The two areas are known as **Fitou Maritime** and **Haut Fitou** and although it was local politics that split the appellation, the two districts produce different-style wines. Why? Yes, you've guessed it. Terroir!

Haut Fitou is a remote and mountainous part of the Corbières 40 minutes inland from its seaside cousin and set in some of the most rugged and wild corners of Languedoc. As you drive along the winding lanes you will see tiny parcels of ancient vines, their trunks as thick as your thigh, clinging onto the rock-strewn soils. This infertile terrain keeps the yields very low, as do the wild boar that roam these hills and devour the ripening bunches from the vine.

There are four villages in the **Haut Fitou** district and a lot of the production centres around the rugby-playing village of Tauchan. Close to the village is Mont Tauch, a huge grey and white mountain that looms up behind the village, dominating the view. Until the 19th century the village people relied on olive oil and wool to make a living and today there are still olive trees cultivated here and many growing wild on the hillsides amongst the ever-present garrigue. It was during the 1800s that, along with everywhere else in Languedoc, wine became the major focus for income here, and as in other areas vines came to dominate the landscape.

Since the 1930s co-operatives have been very significant in the Fitou appellation, but it is increasingly hard for the growers to make a living from grape growing alone and many of them have taken a second job or are getting out of wine growing altogether. The younger generation are not following in their fathers' and grandfathers' footsteps and in the past ten years the volume of wine has fallen by 40%. Unfortunately there is still a struggle for those who remain, as much of the wine is destined for the UK supermarket shelves where it seems the only buying criterion is price. As the fall in production continues the landscape will alter significantly over the next decade as more vines are abandoned and the garrigue takes over. Perhaps some of these vineyards will be bought by new vignerons or by existing independent producers who are already making small quantities of superb wines which they hand-sell to restaurants, specialist shops and wine-loving holiday makers at the cellar door.

I love to take the scenic drive from Tauchan to the village of Fitou in the **Maritime** terroir. You begin by heading to **Château d'Aguilar** sitting on a hill overlooking the town. It was a royal fortress during the reign of St Louis and became one of the 'five sons of the city of Carcassonne', the sturdy castles that guarded the old border between France and Catalonia. It's a wonderful ruin to explore and a perfect place for a picnic with its exceptional panoramic views of the entire region. From here you join the road to the village of Vingrau, which takes you through some breathtaking scenery as you climb out of the valley and eventually come to the plateau with its low pines and not a vine in sight – it's too high. You descend into the village of Vingrau and have now passed into the Roussillon. You may be tempted to stop here and taste the produce of the fine wine makers this village is famed for, but if you're intent on reaching Fitou you will continue through the village and, avoiding the right turn to Tautavel, climb up the hill out of the valley. On your right is the Tautavel circus, an amazing horseshoe-shaped valley, filled with vines and with a stunning backdrop of the Pyrenees.

Once you've climbed to the top of the hill, look out for a left turn to the village of Opoul-Périllos. I don't know if this is a deliberate play on words and I hope you like adventures for this road does seem a little perilous as it climbs and winds its way through this rocky terrain.

At Opoul-Périllos you will see a sign for Fitou and taking this road you will soon arrive at this little village, which does not have a lot to shout about but is a good place to stretch your legs, take in the castle and perhaps taste some wine.

Fitou Maritime, as the name suggests, is closer to the sea and enjoys a much warmer and milder climate and the wines mimic these attributes being softer, much easier to drink and in general have much less ageing potential.

AOP Fitou

This appellation is for red wine only and was the first appellation for dry red wine in Languedoc, formed in 1948. Fitou has two growing areas: Fitou Maritime has clay/limestone soils and Haut Fitou limestone/sandstone soils. The wine must be a blend of Carignan, Grenache and Syrah plus Mourvèdre if the wine maker wishes.

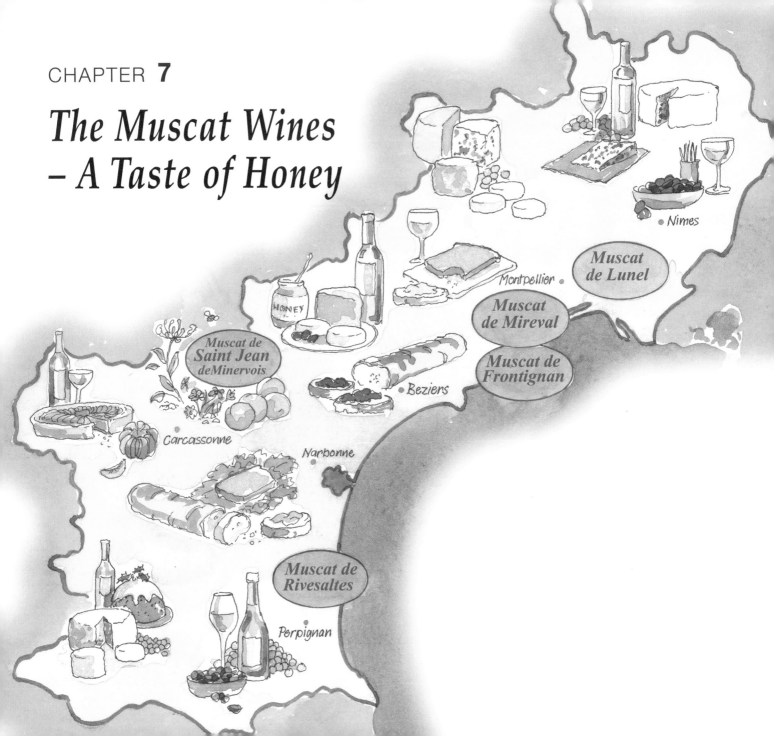

CHAPTER **7**

The Muscat Wines – A Taste of Honey

Muscat de Lunel

Muscat de Mireval

Muscat de Frontignan

Muscat de Saint Jean deMinervois

Muscat de Rivesaltes

Nîmes

Montpellier

Béziers

Carcassonne

Narbonne

Perpignan

HONEY

It's traditional to enjoy a glass of Muscat as an aperitif, called apéro in France. It is the perfect match for salty olives and tapenade but it's also delicious with blue cheese such as Languedoc's delicious Bleu des Causses or Roquefort, or try goat's cheese smeared on crusty French bread and drizzled with honey. Heavenly!

The Muscat grape has been growing around the Mediterranean for many centuries and was known to the ancient Greeks and Romans. It's heavily perfumed and produces wines of the same character. It is the only grape that produces wine that tastes and smells of grapes. There are at least four types of Muscat grape in the world but in the Languedoc-Roussillon only two are used, Muscat Blanc à Petits Grains and Muscat d'Alexandria. The best of the bunch is the Petits Grains and it's the one used to make all four of Languedoc's AOP Muscat wines, leaving the other for Roussillon to use.

Dry Muscat has started to become fashionable and it can be delicious; however, some Muscats seem to lose their magic when the sugar is not present. There is not an appellation for dry Muscat, so it will be labelled as either IGP or Vin du France.

The AOPs for Muscat in Languedoc-Roussillon are all a type of wine called **Vins Doux Naturels**, which translates as 'naturally sweet wine'. This is an ancient style of wine and is found all across the south of France and in parts of Spain. **Vins Doux Naturels** were the invention of an alchemist called Arnaud de Villeneuve who lived in Montpellier in 1285. He discovered the art of 'mutage', or fortifying fermenting juice, which produced wines that were stable enough to undergo long journeys and sea voyages. Port is also produced using mutage; however, the process was invented in Languedoc long before the Portuguese created their famous fortified wine.

To make **Vins Doux Naturels** the grapes are harvested when they are very ripe and must contain a minimum of 252 g/l of sugar or a potential alcohol level of 14.8%. The fermentation starts, and when the yeast has eaten enough of the sugar to reach about 6% ABV the fermenting juice is fortified. This is done by adding neutral grape spirit and bringing the alcohol level up to a minimum of 15% and a maximum of 18% ABV. The yeast is knocked out by the level of alcohol and cannot continue to eat the sugar and therefore you are left with a sweet, alcoholic wine that must have a minimum of 110 g of sugar per litre.

There is one appellation for Muscat in the Roussillon and four in the Languedoc, and these are amongst the oldest appellations in the region. The most famous of them in Languedoc is **AOP Muscat de Frontignan**, found on the coast close to Montpellier. Indeed so famous was this wine that its name became a synonym for the Muscat grape. Many of the vines are planted close to the coast where they ripen well and produce rich, powerful, viscous wines with tropical flavours.

Languedoc-Roussillon Muscat Wines

All the sweet Muscat wines of Languedoc are made with the grape known as Muscat Blanc à Petits Grains and the ones from the Roussillon use Muscat d'Alexandria as well. They are all Vin Doux Naturels and are made by fortifying them with neutral grape spirit during fermentation leaving them sweet and with alcohol levels above 15%.

AOP Muscat de Mireval almost adjoins Frontignan on its eastern side where the vines meet the sea and bathe in the gentle, humid sea breezes rolling in on summer mornings. This gives freshness to the vines and along with the stony soils produces medium-bodied wines that are cleaner and crisper in comparison to some other Muscat wines.

The town of Lunel, which calls itself the City of Muscat, is halfway between Montpellier and Nîmes where the soils are infertile and stony. **AOP Muscat du Lunel** is lightish and fairly refreshing. Its claim to fame is that it was sent to comfort Napoleon during his incarceration on the island of St Helena.

The final Muscat of Languedoc is **AOP Muscat de Saint-Jean-de-Minervois** and is the freshest and most delicate of the Languedoc Muscats. The village of Saint-Jean-de-Minervois is a tiny commune in the far north-east of the Minervois and borders the Saint-Chinian appellation.

The vineyards have been hacked out of the garrigue and are planted on startlingly white limestone soils that cover the red clay below. I remember my first visit to this village. It was spring time and the sky was a glorious azure blue with not a cloud to be seen. As I came over the brow of the hill I was faced with what looked like snow-covered vineyards. It was in fact the white gravel soils that gave the illusion that it had been snowing! This is a limestone plateau and piled up on the edge of the vineyards are limestone boulders blown from the ground with dynamite by farmers searching for soil in which to plant the vines. Much of the rock has been put to use building walls and capitelles so white they look like igloos.

The hills are smothered in vines and garrigue and the wild flowers bloom nearly all year round in the mild climate here. The air is clean and fresh and mingles with the scents of the garrigue. For me it's a little corner of paradise. Of all the Muscats produced in Languedoc-Roussillon these are my favourites. They're different to the others and of course it's all due to the terroir! The white limestone and the altitude of over 200 m are the main influences. They give the wine a crisp freshness and add a delicacy that some Muscats lack. The nose has a perfume of freshly picked roses, honeysuckle and fresh grapes and the palate is a sweet floral honey with apricots, peaches and grapes.

This is a tiny appellation so wherever you are in the world, if you are offered a glass of Muscat de Saint-Jean-de-Minervois, you will know it was made by one of just seven producers!

The village of Saint-Jean-de-Minervois is made up of a handful of cottages, a few wineries, a small church, the co-operative winery and next door the old school house, now a country auberge. Bridget and Patrick are the patrons, she the cook and he front of house, and we dine in the old classroom with its walls festooned with black-and-white photographs of the pupils who learnt their lessons here. Bridget is a fine cook, always using local, seasonal fresh produce to create traditional Languedoc dishes such as her famous cassoulet.

Brigitte Grau's Cassoulet Recipe – Restaurant L'Auberge de L'École

This recipe for cassoulet comes from my grandmother, Elise. Every meal she cooked was a celebration, and every recipe had a story. I would sit near the fire whenever she cooked, listening, learning, and I absolutely believe this is where my love of food and cooking started.

Ingredients to feed four people
400 g of white beans
Tomato purée
One onion, and 3 fat cloves of garlic
4 confit duck legs
50 g of bacon or pancetta, cubed
Toulouse sausage
Herbs de Provence, thyme, and bay leaves
Breadcrumbs

Prepare the white beans by soaking them overnight in plenty of water and a little baking soda. The next day, rinse them thoroughly – two or three times – and then cook them in lots of boiling water; when they're tender, they're ready!

Assembling the Cassoulet
In a large oven-proof casserole dish, gently sauté the onions and garlic in a tablespoon of duck fat until softened but not browned, add the bacon and cook until the fat has rendered down, then add the Toulouse sausage and cook through. Add the tomato purée and herbs, and stir all the ingredients thoroughly to incorporate all the flavours. Cook uncovered in a low oven (120°C), for two hours. Remember to stir after an hour. By this time, the cassoulet should be creamy and unctuous.

Once you've achieved a creamy thick cassoulet, add the confit duck legs, bury them in the beans and return to the oven to heat through the duck. Just before serving add the breadcrumbs, and pop under a grill until bubbling and toasty.

AOP Muscat de Rivesaltes is mainly produced in the Roussillon. It was much sought after in the 14th century when it was made by drying the grapes to concentrate the sugar or even adding honey for a nectar-style wine. It is the only appellation for Muscat in the Roussillon but can actually be produced anywhere in the department of the Pyrénées-Orientales, as well as across the border in the southern part of the Aude around Fitou. The wine can be a blend of both Muscat d'Alexandrie and Muscat Blanc à Petits Grains and is much more viscous and powerful than the Languedoc Muscats. The wines should be drunk very cold and also when young – this is not a wine for ageing as it will lose what freshness it has and become dull and lifeless.

Muscat de Noël, like Beaujolais Nouveau, is released on the third Thursday in November after the harvest and in time for the Christmas season. It is one of the lightest styles of Muscat made here due to the fact that it is made mainly with Muscat Blanc à Petits Grains and is definitely not for ageing.

Cheese

Languedoc-Roussillon produces wonderful cheese, most of which is made from ewe's or goat's milk or even a blend of them both. Some are quite famous such as Roquefort made in the Cevennes from ewe's milk and Pélardon, also from those mountains but this time made with goat's milk. These little round cheeses are delicious and perfect for a picnic. The Pélardon and other chèvre are sold as 'frais', meaning 'fresh'; they are very mild and creamy and only a day or so old. When this cheese has matured for a week it is called 'demi-frais' and now has more flavour and is less moist. After a further week or two the cheese is named 'demi-sec', meaning 'half-dry', and the

flavour has built considerably and the texture is drier. The last stage is called 'sec' and this cheese is completely dry and extremely strong in flavours.

Noilly Prat – the classic Vermouth for making Martini cocktails.

Languedoc is the home of Noilly Prat which hails from Marseillan, the pretty little fishing village set amongst the Picpoul de Pinet vineyards. The Picpoul grape is used to make this beautifully dry vermouth along with another neutral variety called Terret. The recipe is secret and dates back to 1813 when Joseph Noilly developed France's first Vermouth. The Prat part of the name (and yes you do pronounce the T) comes from son-in-law Claudius Prat an Englishman who married mademoiselle Noilly and along with her brother took the company to great heights.

Vermouth is a herb flavoured fortified wine. At Noilly Prat after the wines are made they are then fortified with grape spirit and then put into barrel. Some of them are aged indoors in a room called the Chai des Mistelles and others are aged outside in the elements in what is known as L'Enclos. After the maturation period the wines are blended and then the herbs and spices of the secret recipe are added and the wines are left to macerate in La Salle de Secrets.

You can visit Noilly Prat in Marsellan all year round.

CHAPTER 8

The Roussillon Pyrénées-Oriental

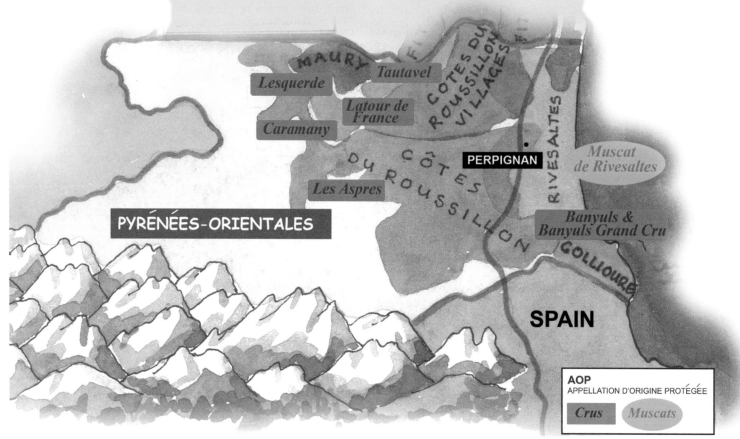

MAURY

Tautavel

Lesquerde

Latour de France

Caramany

CÔTES DU ROUSSILLON VILLAGES

RIVESALTES

PERPIGNAN

Muscat de Rivesaltes

CÔTES DU ROUSSILLON

Les Aspres

PYRÉNÉES-ORIENTALES

Banyuls & Banyuls Grand Cru

COLLIOURE

SPAIN

AOP
APPELLATION D'ORIGINE PROTÉGÉE

Crus   *Muscats*

My overriding impression of the Roussillon is the beautiful mountains and the searing heat. I first visited the area 20 years ago and although at that time I had never set foot in Spain, I felt Roussillon had a distinctly Iberian feel to it and I was right. In 1659 the Treaty of the Pyrenees was signed, which brought an end to the Spanish–French conflict, and part of Catalonia became French and was renamed Roussillon. The papers may have been signed and the maps changed, but still today it's a Catalan heart that beats in the chests of the people who live here.

This is France's most southerly outpost and its hottest and driest region, with its capital city Perpignan wearing the badge for the windiest and driest city in France. The city boasts some magnificent 13th- and 14th-century buildings. Amongst them is the oldest royal residence in France. However it was not originally French and is called the Palace of the Kings of Mallorca.

Looming high above the city is Le Canigou, which holds a special place in the hearts and minds of the Catalan people who call it the sacred mountain. It is not the highest peak of the Pyrenees mountain chain but one of the most dramatic, and here close to Perpignan is where the mountains meet and sink into the Mediterranean Sea. The mountains dominate the landscape and are high enough in places for snow to remain all year round. The height of the mountain range is exaggerated by its location, butting up to the Roussillon plain which is extremely flat and extends inland from the sea. The traditional produce of the region is still found here in abundance; wine was always part of the commerce of the region but also olive oil, cork oaks which grow naturally here and fruit such as apricots, peaches and cherries.

Due to the geological forces that created the Pyrenees, The Roussillon contains just about every soil type you can think of and due to the rippling landscape and blistering heat there is an abundance of different terroirs. All these factors work to produce a range of wines that have elaborate complexity and minerality.

Roussillon is bounded by mountains to the north, west and south with the Mediterranean closing the circle to the east. Three river valleys traverse the landscape west to east, the Agly, the Têt and the Tech, and it's around these rivers that the majority of the wines are grown. The Roussillon covers a much smaller area than the Languedoc; however, more than half of the wine produced here is AOP and only a miniscule amount is IGP.

The largest appellation in the region goes by the name of **AOP Côtes du Roussillon** and stretches across the entire region, encompassing a wide range of terroirs and producing an equally wide range of wine styles in all 3 colours.

AOP Côtes du Roussillon

This appellation is for red, rosé and white wine and is produced across the Roussillon on a variety of soils including clay, limestone, schist, granite, gneiss and iron rich red clay. The red and rosé is a blend of Carignan, Grenache Noir, Syrah, Mourvèdre, Cinsault and Lladoner Pelut. Producers can add up to 30% of the white grape Macabeu into the rosé if they choose to. The white is a blend that can contain Grenache Blanc, Grenache Gris, Macabeu, Roussanne, Marsanne, Vermentino and Tourbat.

There is just one cru in the Côtes du Roussillon called **AOP Côtes du Roussillon Les Aspres** which is a recent addition and found in the most southerly part of the region.

AOP Côtes du Roussillon Les Aspres

This is the only cru in the Côtes du Roussillon and is an appellation is for red wine only. The vines are grown on gravel, galets roulés and clay/limestone and the wines are a blend of Carignan, Grenache, Syrah and Mourvèdre.

The next appellation in the Roussillon hierarchy is **AOP Côtes du Roussillon Villages** which is located between the Agly and the Têt river valleys. It's in this area that many passionate and talented wine makers have resurrected abandoned vineyards and breathed new life into discarded farms. A lot of them are farming and making wine using organic and biodynamic methods on small plots of seven hectares or less. Many of the vines are old, over 80 years, and some more than 100. At this age the vine lowers its yield considerably, which concentrates the flavours and produces wines of incredible depth and interest.

Many talented wine makers have grouped together in the pretty little village of Calce, which seems to be the epicentre for fine wine production. Here you will find famous wine makers such as Gauby and Olivier Pithon. The day I visited I arrived at lunch time, so I headed for the little café-restaurant in the square. The menu was simple and cheap at only €13.50 but the cheapest glass of wine was €20 – we were in expensive wine country, but my goodness was it good!

The Roussillon – Pyrénées-Orientales

Côtes du Roussillon Villages is a red wine appellation only but white wines are grown here too and are labelled either IGP or just plain Côtes du Roussillon without the word 'Village' in the title. I have found some white wine gems here as it's the sort of wine that appeals to my palate. I like mineral, bone-dry whites full of character and an underlying richness. I am also a big fan of Carignan and it was in this area that I first encountered the rare Carignan Gris being used to make a superb white wine. If you're lucky you will also find Carignan Blanc.

AOP Côtes du Roussillon Villages

This is an appellation is for red wine only and is located between the Agly and the Têt river valleys and encompasses 32 villages. The soils are grey and black schist, limestone, iron-rich red clay, gneiss, granite and galets roulés and the wines are a blend of Grenache Noir, Carignan, Lladoner Pelut, Syrah and Mourvèdre.

AOP Côtes du Roussillon Villages Crus

Some of the villages in these valleys have been awarded cru status; there are 4 of them and each one has chosen the most famous village to be the figurehead for their cru: **Caramany**, **Lesquerde**, **Latour de France** and **Tautavel**. I particularly like the wines from this last appellation which are grown in the villages of Vingrau and Tautavel which are located on the Roussillon side of the Corbières hills, in some of the most scenic landscapes. The vines are planted on the gentle slopes of the beautiful horseshoe-shaped valley called the Circus of

Vingrau. It's a unique limestone rock formation, the only one of its kind in the world, filled with a patchwork display of vines surrounded by garrigue. The sea of vines is bathed in sunlight and reaches intense ripeness which produces wines that are powerfully concentrated, perfumed, herby and full-bodied, with great depth of flavour and richness. These wines have the longest ageing potential of the region.

On one side of the horseshoe the pretty village of Vingrau is home to some splendid producers and close by is the Arago cave where the remains of Tautavel Man, who lived here 450,000 years ago, were discovered.

AOP Côtes du Roussillon Villages Crus
Caramany, Lesquerde, Latour de France and Tautavel

These cru appellations within Côtes du Roussillon Villages are for red wines only. Some are grown at higher altitude than others but the soils are very similar and include schist, clay and limestone and in Lesquerde granite and gneiss. The wines must be a blend using Grenache Noir, Lladoner Pelut, Syrah and Carignan. Mourvèdre is allowed in Latour de France but not in the other three.

The Cathar Crusade

The Cathar religion spread to many parts of Europe during the 12th and 13th centuries, but it was in Languedoc where it flourished and eventually was openly practised. In those days Languedoc was not part of France and was not a kingdom with the usual hierarchical society. Instead it had a feudal system of many lords holding allegiances in various directions. Law and order was in the hands of the Count of Toulouse and the Pope had ordered him to stamp out Catharism. For various reasons, not least that some of his family were Cathars, he did not carry out the Popes orders.

Cathars believed there were two Gods. The God of the Old Testament was an angry and wrathful God who punished people such as Adam & Eve for making a mistake and would not allow Moses to enter the Promised Land. He was seen as evil and as the creator of the Earth so too was this place and in the context of living conditions in those days it must have felt like hell on earth sometimes. The God in heaven was thought of as the God of Love and the people believed that Jesus had come to earth to tell them how to get to heaven and be with this God. They believed Jesus had tried to teach people to be good Christians, to love thy neighbour, not to kill or harm and to live a humble life, living from what you can do with your own hands. They believed if you did not follow this way of life, when you died you would be re-incarnated back onto this evil Earth.

As Catharism took hold in Languedoc the Pope tried to control the people and bring them back to the Catholic faith but his efforts failed and he realised he needed armed men to crush the Cathars in Languedoc. Eventually he persuaded the King of France to join him in a Holy War, a Crusade against Catharism. The King wanted Languedoc to be part of his realm and saw the Crusade as the way to achieve his desire. He raised a huge army led by the Dukes of France and Warrior Catholic Churchmen who marched on Languedoc.

The first siege took place in 1208 at the city of Béziers and was expected to take many weeks but invasion of the city was made easy on the first day. A group of lads came out to mock the troops who chased them back into the city through the open gate. It was at this point that the Cistercian abbot and commander of the crusade Arnaud Amaury, was reported to have been asked how to tell Cathar from Catholic. His reply was "Kill them all - the Lord will recognise His own". The slaughter of 20,000 people, men, woman and children in Béziers was the beginning of the end of Catharism.

Simon De Montfort, a knight from Northern France showed his leadership at the siege of Carcassonne. After the death of Raymond Roger Trencavel, Simon De Montfort became Viscount of Carcassonne and led the crusade for 10 years until his death at the siege of Toulouse. His son took over but was not the fighter his father had been and eventually returned to France and presented the King with all the Languedoc lands his father had won. Languedoc now belonged to France and the King would eventually claim it.

By 1229 Catharism had been sent underground but it had not been wiped out. Pope Gregory IX appointed the Dominicans to begin the Inquisition. They set up tribunals and over the following years they winkled out suspected heretics and any Cathars found were burned at the stake.

Many of the Bons Hommes and Bonnes Femmes, the leaders of the faith and often referred to as Perfects, went into hiding. They took refuge in castles that had previously been built to guard the frontier between Languedoc and Catalonia. One of these places is called Montségur, a stone fortress built on top of a huge fist shaped mountain and it's here in 1243 that the last siege of the Cathar crusade began. It lasted 10 months and when it ended those who refused to recant their faith were put to death on a huge pyre below the castle.

Although Montségur was not the final stand it was a huge disaster for the Cathar faith and heralded its end, although some say there are still Cathars in Languedoc to this day.

AOP Maury

Not far from Tautavel is the village of Maury in the Agly valley, which is skirted by a row of impressive limestone bluffs called Grau. Here you will find the castles of Quéribus and Peyrepertuse, which long ago formed the defensive line for the now-defunct border between France and Catalonia. Château de Quéribus sits on top of the Grau of Maury and rises high to cast its shadow over the vines growing on the black schist soils below. Nestled in the valley is the village of Maury, which gives its name to some of the most delicious sweet red wines I have ever come across.

The climate here is intensely hot, dry and often very windy. The vines are grown very low to protect them from the wind that reduces their yield and shrivels the grapes, which concentrates the sugars, acid and flavours. Grenache is very at home in this climate, where it thrives and shrugs off the heat without batting an eyelid to produce sweet red wines that are the chefs' favourite pairing for chocolate. **AOP Maury** is the smallest of the Vins Doux Naturels appellations in Roussillon. I would describe it as a little like a Ruby Port but not so fiery, often less sugary and slightly lower in alcohol with flavours of smoky raspberries, chocolate and tobacco. Although fairly rare you can also find white Maury. It tastes of honey, apricots and quince and is delicious with hard cheeses as well as blue cheese.

Château Peyreperteuse

AOP Maury

Sweet Maury is a Vin Doux Naturels and therefore a fortified wine and is mainly red with a small amount of white also made. The very low yielding vines are grown on black schist soils. The reds must be a minimum of 75% Grenache and some are 100% but other grapes can be blended including Carignan, Syrah and surprisingly up to 10% of the white grape Macabeu can be included. White Maury can be made from Grenache Blanc, Grenache Gris, Macabeu, Tourbat, Muscat d'Alexandrie and Muscat Blanc à Petits Grains.

Up until the vintage of 2011 all Maury was sweet but now producers have a new appellation for dry ('sec') red Maury. It's a move to help the growers eke out a living on this tough landscape, as sweet wine is not as popular these days and it is hoped that a dry wine will save the co-operative dominated village.

AOP Maury Sec

This appellation is for dry red wine only grown on black schist and made from between 60 and 80% Grenache plus Carignan, Syrah and Mourvèdre.

AOP Rivesaltes

The Roussillon is well known for the production of sweet, fortified wines such as Maury and Banyuls which it has been making for many centuries and they are still at the heart of the production here. They fell from favour but in later years we have seen a revival and I for one am delighted as I adore them.

AOP Rivesaltes are Vins Doux Naturels grown mainly on the Roussillon plain around the town of Rivesaltes which is just north of Perpignan. The town is twinned with Clitheroe, a Lancashire town in the north of England and quite an unlikely sibling. The two towns have very little in common where wine making is concerned unless you count the presence of the top-class wine merchants D. Byrne & Co. in Clitheroe, who are well worth a visit.

The red soils of the flat Roussillon plain sandwiched between the Mediterranean Sea and the Pyrenees are planted with vines, fruit and olive trees. The fierce unrelenting heat bakes the soil and dust storms are commonly whipped up by the almost constant wind. In these conditions the grapes shrivel and dry on the vines producing grapes with high sugar content, making them ideal for sweet wine production.

There are quite a number of styles of Rivesaltes wine. They range from fruity and reasonably light, ideal as an aperitif, to deeply concentrated and complex to finish a meal or to accompany strong cheeses. Some are named after their colour:

- **Rosé**, which is a new addition to the appellation, introduced from the 2011 vintage. It has flavours of strawberry, raspberry, grenadine and redcurrants and should be served chilled as a delicious aperitif.

- **Grenat** means 'garnet', which is the colour of this wine. Serve it chilled as an aperitif or try it with a chocolate dessert!

- **Tuilé** takes its name from the colour of baked terracotta tiles: reddish brown with hints of orange and yellow. Flavours of prunes, quince, tobacco, coffee and chocolate make this a delicious match with strong cheeses accompanied by quince jelly.

- **Ambré** is a deep amber colour and is often a very complex wine with aromas and flavours of Seville oranges, crystallised fruit, hazelnuts and almonds. It is wonderful with cheeses and some orange-based desserts.

And some are named after their maturity:

- **Hors d'âge** means 'beyond age'. The wine is a minimum of five years old and has flavours of prunes and raisins, walnuts and almonds.

- **Rancio** is a faded brown colour and has flavours of caramel and toffee.

AOP Rivesaltes

Rivesaltes are Vin Doux Naturels wines grown on varied soils including clay/limestone, schist, sand, granite and gneiss. There are quite a few styles:

Rosé and Grenat are made using 100% Grenache.
Tuilé is a blend of Grenache Noir, Grenache Gris, Grenache Blanc, Macabeu and Malvoisie.
Ambré is a white wine the colour of amber due to oxidative ageing and is a blend made from Grenache Gris, Grenache Blanc, Macabeu, Malvoisie, Muscat Blanc à Petits Grains and Muscat d'Alexandrie.

Collioure and Banyuls

Collioure is a charming seaside village that has a great and important history going back beyond Roman times. It and the village of Banyuls are located on the dramatic Côtes Vermeille. The town of Collioure was a source of inspiration for artists such as Picasso and Matisse who, along with others, immortalised the small Catalan harbour with its church, seemingly built in the sea.

You need to have someone else doing the driving when you follow the ledge-hugging corniche road in order to take in the spectacular views on both sides. Below you on one side glistens the Mediterranean Sea and on the other the vertiginous terraced vineyards cascading down the steep hillsides.

There are two appellations in this area, one for dry red, white and rosé named **AOP Collioure** and the other for the sweet fortified **AOP Banyuls.** The vines for both these wines are grown on the same footprint, on terroir that is some of the most dramatic in France. The vines are planted on dramatically inclined, schistous slopes that spill down to the sea and are so steep that tractors can't enter the vineyards; all the work is carried out by man and mule. The climate is scorching hot but the sea and frequent wind help to alleviate the tireless heat. It hardly ever rains here but when it does the heavens open, so drainage channels have been dug in the vineyards to deal with the deluge of rainwater in a bid to avoid too much soil erosion.

Banyuls

The red Collioure wines are full-bodied, rich, spicy, savoury and peppery. Many of the vines are old and gnarled and trained low, giving yields that are much reduced due to the harsh terroir. The sunny and breezy conditions keep mildew and rot at bay but the vines struggle to survive as irrigation is not usually practised here and the soils are poor and stony. The Grenache-based white wines are often barrel-fermented, giving body and intense honey and tropical fruit flavours coupled with ozone and iodine characters that evoke the close vicinity of the Mediterranean Sea.

AOP Collioure

This appellation is for red, rosé and white wine. The low yielding vines are growing on grey schist on very steep slopes close to the Mediterranean Sea. The red and rosé is a blend of Grenache, Syrah, Mourvèdre and Carignan and the white wines are made using Grenache Blanc and Grenache Gris.

Collioure

AOP Banyuls

It is often said that a stressed vine will produce the best wine and this is borne out when you taste your first glass of Banyuls. This sweet wine appellation differs from Rivesaltes in that not a hint of Muscat is allowed and most Banyuls wine is red with only a small amount of white wine made. The red wines must contain at least 50% Grenache Noir however many of the vineyards were planted 80 or a hundred years ago and are a blend of all 3 colours of Grenache which are often harvested and fermented at the same time.

There are fundamentally two styles of Banyuls. Traditionally it was matured in glass bonbonnes in the sunshine to achieve what's called a rancio character. This style is still made; it has flavours of caramel, toffee and walnuts and is delicious with a fine aged Manchego cheese. In later years much of the wine has been made to display the youthful heady aromas of macerated red fruits, produced with no oxidation and with minimal ageing; this style is similar to vintage Port.

AOP Banyuls

These Vin Doux Naturels wines are grown in the same place and on the same soils as AOP Collioure. They are made red, rosé and white. The red and rosé must contain a minimum of 50% Grenache Noir and the remainder from Grenache Gris and Grenache Blanc. The whites are made from Grenache Blanc, Grenache Gris, Macabeu and Tourbat.

Banyuls Grand Cru does not refer to a superior terroir as in Burgundy and Alsace. They are wines produced in the best years only and made with deliberate oxidation. They must contain at least 75% Grenache Noir and be aged for a minimum of two and a half years, which is usually well exceeded to produce wines that have flavours of caramel, tobacco, coffee and leather. The varying levels of sweetness can be indicated on the label using terms such as 'sec', 'brut' or 'dry'.

AOP Banyuls Grand Cru

This is an appellation for red Vin Doux Naturels wine is only which are produced in only the best years and is made in an oxidative style. The wine must contain a minimum of 75% Grenache Noir and can also contain Grenache Gris and Grenache Blanc.

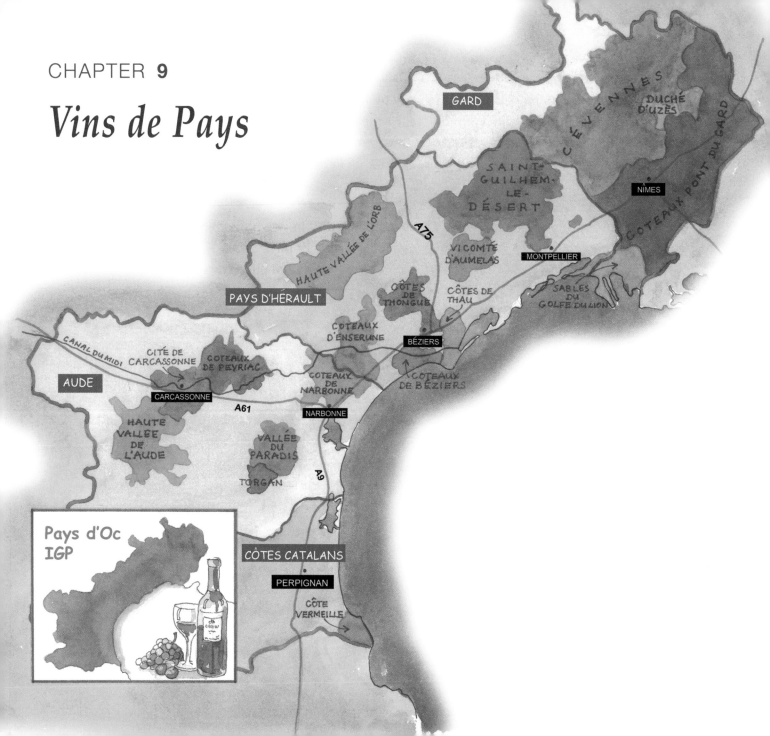

CHAPTER 9

Vins de Pays

GARD

CÉVENNES

DUCHÉ D'UZÈS

SAINT-GUILHEM-LE-DÉSERT

NÎMES

COTEAUX PONT DU GARD

A75

HAUTE VALLÉE DE L'ORB

VICOMTÉ D'AUMELAS

MONTPELLIER

CÔTES DE THONGUE

CÔTES DE THAU

SABLES DU GOLFE DU LION

PAYS D'HÉRAULT

COTEAUX D'ENSERUNE

BÉZIERS

CANAL DU MIDI

CITÉ DE CARCASSONNE

COTEAUX DE PEYRIAC

COTEAUX DE NARBONNE

COTEAUX DE BÉZIERS

AUDE

CARCASSONNE

A61

NARBONNE

HAUTE VALLÉE DE L'AUDE

VALLÉE DU PARADIS

A9

TORGAN

Pays d'Oc IGP

CÔTES CATALANS

PERPIGNAN

CÔTE VERMEILLE

When I first started taking an interest in wine I was told the translation of 'Vins de Pays' was 'wines from the countryside', which implied they were the 'peasant' wines of France and would be rustic and simple. I now realise that the use of the word 'pays' refers to a part of France, a region or a department. For instance, **Vins de Pays d'Oc** are wines from the pay of Languedoc.

In 2009 IGP became the new name for Vins de Pays and in Languedoc that means the wines formerly known as Vins de Pays d'Oc are now called **IGP Pays d'Oc**. IGP is a designation used all over France and there are over 150 in existence but the Languedoc range is the broadest and the most successful of them all. It is the figurehead behind which a revolution in wine-making has taken place and outstanding success achieved. In the past few years there has been a reduction in the amount of wine produced in Languedoc; however at the same time the amount of IGP wine has increased and now accounts for around half of all wine made in Languedoc, although it is less important in Roussillon.The success of the old Vins de Pays proved to be a saviour for the region. It was led by a clear marketing campaign that latched onto consumers' increasing preference for buying wine by grape variety rather than provenance. In the early days the success was based on what I like to call 'Vin de Quaff', in other words simple, fruity wines, named after the grape and at a price that most people can afford. But as the brand strengthened and as wine makers adopted it to label their non-conformist wines, it evolved to include mid-priced and premium wines too.

IGP producers have a list of 30 grape varieties to choose from and can opt to make a mono-varietal wine using just one grape variety, a bi-varietal made from two grape varieties or a blended wine made from three or more grape varieties. As you would expect from a hot region

the majority of IGP wines are red, making up about 60% of production, with rosé and white making up equal shares of about 20% each. International varieties are still the bulk of production with Merlot and Cabernet Sauvignon in pole position and Chardonnay topping the list of whites; however Viognier is also popular and because it's not yet allowed in many appellations nearly all of it is bottled as IGP.

As well as dry wines, for centuries Languedoc made sweet wines using over-ripe grapes or by using a process called passerillage which involves drying the grapes to concentrate the sugar. However, because the appellations for sweet wines in Languedoc are confined to the fortified wines called Vins Doux Naturels, the other traditional methods lapsed. Today these practices have been revived and because there is not an AOP for them, many are bottled as IGP and in some cases as Vin du France. They are made using many different grape varieties including Chenin Blanc, Muscat, Viognier and Sauvignon Blanc to name but a few, and some of the finest examples can rival late harvest wines from other parts of France.

Although, in contrast to AOP, IGP offers more flexibility to the wine maker, there are still strict criteria to adhere to, especially regarding where the wine is grown. The label must state if the wine is **Régional**, **Départental** or **Zonal**.

Régional IGP wines in Languedoc-Roussillon are called **IGP Pays d'Oc**. The grapes for these wines can originate from anywhere within both Languedoc and Roussillon, and as with many New World wines the rules for growing and making are far less strict than for AOP wines and encourage innovation and creativity. These wines are about territory and grape variety rather than the personality of terroir and the art of assemblage. However none of these things are ruled out and the wines still retain a 'Languedoc-Roussillon' character when grown in Pays d'Oc due to the climate. The majority of these wines are single varietal, which has helped make this the most successful IGP in France with exported volume reaching almost twice as much as Bordeaux.

There are three **Départental IGPs** in Languedoc, and each carries the name of the department where the grapes are grown: **IGP d'Aude**, **IGP de l'Hérault**, **IGP de Gard**. In Roussillon the Départental IGP is called **IGP Côtes Catalanes**. Producers are a little hesitant to use a Départental IGP as it's not so well known to the outside world as the IGP Pays d'Oc brand and may hinder sales, and this is why this designation only accounts for about 25% of output.

Zonal IGP refers to wines that come from a district within a department and there are 23 in Languedoc-Roussillon, all making red, white and rosé wines.

The Gard

The landscape in the Gard is one of contrast. In the north are the Cévennes Mountains, towards the coast the marshy lowlands of the Camargue and sandwiched in-between is a garrigue-smothered plateau, and each area has varying degrees of Mediterranean climate. Here producers of IGP wine can choose to label their wines **IGP de Gard** or opt to use the name of the zone it grows within.

There are four Zonal IGPs here and beginning in the east is **IGP Coteaux du Pont du Gard**, a large and relatively flat area that encompasses the famous Roman aqueduct of the same name. The far eastern edge of this IGP is close to the Rhône Delta and producers in that part of the Rhône can also choose to use this IGP if they wish. This IGP produces full-bodied reds and lighter whites and rosés. In the north you will find **IGP Cévennes** taking its name from the nearby stretch of mountains which form the beginning of the Massif Central. This area is cooler than many parts of the Languedoc and the resulting wines are much more elegant, fresh and aromatic. **IGP Duché d'Uzès** is located in the middle of the department where the handsome town of Uzès sits. With quality in mind, the maximum permitted yields for these wines are much lower than normally allowed and the area has recently applied for AOP status. **IGP Sables de Camargue/Sables du Golfe du Lion** is situated in an exceptional location where vines are planted in the sandy soils of the Camargue close to the Mediterranean Sea and the salt lagoons found along that part of the coastline. The zone is found near the pretty seaside town of Les Saintes Maries de la Mer, where legend has it Mary Magdalene first set foot in France. Le Cap d'Agde is also in this area and is well known for the production of very pale rosé.

The Hérault

The Hérault is the largest producer of IGP wines in the Languedoc, accounting for 40% of the 50 million gallons of **IGP Pays d'Oc** produced annually from across the region. On top of this the department also produces 20,000 gallons of **IGP Pays d'Hérault**, with much of it being single varietal made from the international varieties and priced at entry level.

The Hérault has eight zones. **IGP Coteaux de Béziers** is the new name for the zone previously called Coteaux du Libron, surrounding the city of Béziers. The vast majority of wines made under this IGP are single varietal and sold at entry level price points. **IGP Coteaux d'Ensérune** is home to Maraussan, which is one of the first cave co-operatives built in Languedoc. The zone is located west of Béziers and the vines are planted below the ancient pre-Roman hill town called Oppidum d'Ensérune. It is well worth a visit and if you climb to the top and look north you will see a strange circular set of fields that look like a launch pad for an alien spaceship. This was once a saltwater lake and many of the families that cultivate this land today are descendants of the people who drained the étang in the 13th century.

    IGP Côtes de Thau covers a similar footprint to AOP Picpoul de Pinet around the salty Étang du Thau where co-operative wineries are very important. Not all but most of the production of this IGP is white wine made from the ubiquitous Sauvignon Blanc, Chardonnay and Viognier grapes. **IGP Côtes de Thongue** is a large zone sitting between the towns of Faugères, Pézenas and Béziers. The landscape is interesting and handsome with low rolling hillsides. It is home to many good independent producers and a handful of co-operatives and much of the good fruity red wine is destined for export.

IGP Haute Vallée de l'Orb is a small zone located in much the same place as Saint-Chinian Roquebrun, tucked into the hills close to the Cévennes and the Black Mountains. Much of this area has schist soils, but slotted between are patches of other soils where grapes destined for IGP are often grown. These fragrant wines are well thought of and have good minerality and freshness. **IGP Saint-Guilhem-le-Désert** is small but highly regarded and home to some of the most famous producers of IGP wine in the whole of Languedoc. The zone is within the Terrasses du Larzac and Pic Saint-Loup terroirs and includes the village of Aniane where Mas de Daumas Gassac create their Bordeaux-influenced wines. You may also come across some wines labelled as **Saint-Guilhem-le-Désert Val de Montferrand,** which refers to a sub-zone and is often used by Pic Saint-Loup producers to label their white wines. **Vicomté d'Aumelas** is an IGP found between Montpellier and Béziers making light and fruity reds.

The switch to IGP has streamlined things a little in the Hérault department but there is still a long list of sub-zones (listed below) that can be appended to IGP Pays d'Hérault. Here are a few: La Benovie, Caux, Collines de la Moure, Côtes de Brian and Coteaux de Murviel.

The Aude

The Aude is home to many famous appellations such as the Corbières, Limoux and much of the Minervois. It has quite a varied landscape containing dozens of terroirs and the wines produced on them are equally assorted in style. White wine is made here but the vast majority is red and rosé made from many different grape varieties including local and international grapes and some that you may not have come across before such as Chasan which is said to be a cross involving Chardonnay.

IGP d'Aude has seven zones, all making red, rosé and white wines. As is indicated by the name, the grapes for **IGP Cité de Carcassonne** are grown around this impressive medieval walled town. **IGP Côteaux de Peyriac** is found in the centre of the Minervois and on a gentle rolling landscape close to the beautiful village of Caunes-Minervois. Much of the wine is red made using local or international varieties and I have also come across some unexpected varieties such as the Italian grape Nebbiolo and the Spanish Tempranillo. There are also some good Viognier and Chardonnay made in this area. The **IGP Coteaux de Narbonne** wines are mainly located between the city and the coast and are a source for good Cabernet Sauvignon and Merlot as well as wines made from local varieties. It's good hunting ground for wines with a similar character to those of AOP La Clape as much of it is grown on the same terroir.

IGP Le Pays Cathare is a name chosen to take advantage of the interest shown in the Cathars and **Haute Vallée de l'Aude** produces excellent Pinot Noir, Sauvignon Blanc and Chardonnay.

The romantically named **IGP Vallée du Paradis** is set in rugged landscape in the heart of the Corbières. Close by is **IGP Vallée du Torgan**, an IGP with a history that goes back to 1987. Both these IGPs produce highly regarded well-made wines with plenty of personality.

IGP d'Aude can be grown across the entire department and here, as in the Hérault, there are some sub-zones that can append their name if they wish; here are just a few: **Côtes de Lastours**, **Pays de Cucugnan** and **La Côte Révée**.

Pyrénées-Orientales

As mentioned earlier The Roussillon produces far more AOP wine than IGP and therefore it's no surprise that there are only two Zonal IGPs in this region. However both are good hunting ground for quality wine usually produced from low-yielding vines and often made by some of the finest producers in the area. **IGP Côtes Catalanes** is made across the whole of Roussillon apart from around Banyuls and Collioure. All 3 colours are available and often the reds are made using local varieties grown on the better terroir. You will find international varieties too which are often grown on  the flatter land. The omnipresent Chardonnay is there but I think it's too hot to make good examples so I look out for white wines made from Grenache Blanc and Gris, Marsanne, Roussanne and Vermentino.

The most southerly IGP in France is called **IGP Côtes Vermeille** which takes its name from the pink rocks that make up the coastline around the villages of Collioure and Banyuls where the grapes for this IGP are grown. The wines can be any of the 3 colours and are usually of high quality and often made from local varieties.

CHAPTER **10**

The Future

Languedoc-Roussillon is poised, ready for the next stage in its evolution and relishing the challenges to come. It's been an interesting journey so far and many people feel the best is yet to come. Shrugging off the reputation for quantity over quality has been a long, slow process but it is happening and those who discover the exceptional wines of the Languedoc-Roussillon know the future is bright.

I believe the next 20 years will see the quantity of wine produced here lowering still further and we will see the demise of co-operative wineries that have chosen not to follow the road to quality. I hope we don't lose them all; they are an important part of the history and society here and many are trying hard to raise the quality of the wine they produce. As some co-operatives go out of business so the landscape will change as vineyards are uprooted and either left for the garrigue to devour or re-planted with other crops.

I'm sure IGP Pays d'Oc will continue to flourish and will be recognised as a quality wine designation that encompasses many types of wine. It will shrug off its image of being cheap and cheerful; it no longer deserves that.

The hierarchy of appellations will continue to emerge and the majority of the sub-appellations of AOP Languedoc will gain their own stand-alone recognition and new ones will also appear. I believe more crus and village appellations will emerge from the large district appellations of Minervois, Corbières and others to highlight the differences in the terroir.

I hope restaurant wine lists around the globe will begin to list these wines alongside highly regarded French wines such as Châteauneuf du Pape, Saint-Émilion and Nuits Saint-Georges, which is where they belong. If this recognition comes, as I believe it will, Languedoc-Roussillon will have turned full circle and the wines once exalted in Rome will be back where they belong.

The Illustrator – Jenny Baker

Jenny Baker retired from lecturing in art and design in 2009 and now concentrates on illustration and water colour painting. She divides her time between Ireland, where she has lived for the last thirty-six years, and Caunes-Minervois in France, where she paints the landscape and the flora of the area.

It was here that she met Wendy, who invited her to collaborate on her book. They share an enthusiasm for the landscape of the region and the wine that it produces.

Index of appelations

Vin en Vacances
Vineyard tours in the
Languedoc-Roussillon

If you're planning to visit the beautiful south of France come and join us on one of our very special vineyard tours and let us introduce you to some of the Languedoc-Roussillon's finest wine makers and taste their delicious wines.

We offer a choice of vineyard tours that will immerse you in the French culture, the cuisine, history and of course the wines! Choose from a fabulous range of day trips and wine holidays.

Our tours operate between Carcassonne and Pézenas

How to Arrange Your Tour
To arrange your tour call Wendy on 0033 (0)6 42 33 34 09 (French mobile) or 0044 (0)7880 796786 (English mobile) or email wendy@vinenvacances.com

www.vinenvacances.com